SEX, COLLEGE
& SOCIAL MEDIA

SEX, COLLEGE & SOCIAL MEDIA

A COMMONSENSE GUIDE TO NAVIGATING THE HOOKUP CULTURE

CINDY PIERCE

Cindy Pierce

bibliomotion inc.

First published by Bibliomotion, Inc.
39 Harvard Street
Brookline, MA 02445
Tel: 617-934-2427
www.bibliomotion.com

Printed in the United States of America

Print ISBN 978-1-62956-171-4
E-book ISBN 978-1-62956-172-1
Enhanced E-book ISBN 978-1-62956-173-8

CIP data has been applied for.

For Bruce, Zander, Sadie, and Colter. Thanks for your support and open conversation.

CONTENTS

INTRODUCTION

Over the past ten years I have stumbled, somewhat unwittingly, into the role of social sexuality expert. My first presentations were intended to entertain, with a side of information. After I spoke to my niece's sorority and my nephew's fraternity, I started to get more requests to speak to college students. The significant gaps in students' knowledge about sex became alarmingly evident as I responded to their questions, comments, and concerns.

In sharing their personal stories over the years, college students have provided me with a window of understanding into their social and sexual lives. Groups of women are almost always direct with their questions. I was initially surprised that the men were equally open and willing to engage with me. Because I am a nonjudgmental, informative, auntie-like figure who isn't fazed and stands outside the realm of their social, academic, and family lives, they freely share their doubts, vulnerabilities, or questions about sex. I couldn't turn back from what I learned as I talked to young people about their experiences, which led me to give presentations at high schools and colleges across the country. I speak openly and in depth about sex because I believe that an informed decision increases a young person's chance of staying physically and emotionally healthy.

I was inspired to write this book by the confusion and misinformation I see among college students regarding the basics of sex and sexuality, and by my desire to help young people navigate today's media-influenced hookup culture in the healthiest way possible. If you are like most of the students I meet, you want to get informed without admitting your confusion publicly. Having grown up in an age where information is instantly available, many of you seem to feel that you should be able to figure everything out on your own. But that's not easy when so much misinformation is jumbled together with solid sources in a way that makes it hard to tell them apart—who can you trust?

In this book, I have put together information on the most pressing concerns I hear from college students today: hookup sex, drinking, STIs, contraception, appropriate language and acronyms regarding gender identity and sexual orientation, and how to have better sex and relationships. Along with the facts and figures, I have included quotes and stories that come directly from students your age—some are funny, some are sad, all are informative. My hope is that you can learn from the confused escapades and experiences of your peers, as well as from those who make informed and healthy decisions. I have also recruited experts in various fields who work with college students in different capacities to contribute their wisdom and perspective.

The ongoing input I receive from recent graduates and older college students shaped this book. They speak to me with urgency about how fast our culture is changing, leaving many college students feeling socially and sexually inadequate. They are concerned that so many people just go along with the hookup culture. Many recent graduates hope that students will pay closer attention to advice, guidance, and information offered from older students, as well as from school and community programs, and that these resources will inspire more conscious choices. While this sounds like every adult's advice since the beginning of time, today the messages conveyed through social media speed up and complicate social lives and sexual choices. By sharing information gathered from people who have been where you are, I hope to help you stay grounded and decide what is right for you while you navigate the social terrain of your campus—both online and off.

My goal is to send you forward with the tools you need to have healthy, happy, consensual sex when you are ready, as well as to direct you to better resources than porn, misinformed peers, and WebMD.

Keep this book somewhere close at hand and use it as a reliable, research-based source of information whenever you or a friend should need it.

A final note before we begin: Many of the terms in this book are subject to frequent changes in definition and association. Though I have done my best to be accurate, the definitions I provide here and the ways in which I use certain words may not align with the way they are understood by readers from diverse cultures and regions. Along with improving general understanding, I aim to educate those who seek to interact with greater sensitivity. Please appreciate that goal and do what you can to further that goal by educating others.

1

The Misinformation Age

How the Media Warps Expectations

Today's omnipresent media has had a major impact on what we are conditioned to expect from our bodies, our sexual relationships, and ourselves. This has landed us in what I like to call the "misinformation age"—we are all so overwhelmed with conflicting messages and impossible expectations that it has become very difficult to get to the truth. Many of the questions I have received from students over the years stem from this growing mountain of misinformation; in this chapter, I'll provide answers to some of the most common questions I hear.

Why Is Body Image Such a Problem?

Body image issues continue to grow as the culture feeds messages to consumers at a faster pace through more media than ever before. The relentless messaging that you, whether you are male or female, are not enough—not attractive enough, not hot enough, not endowed enough, and so on—is a marketing ploy that continues to sell products. According to a study done in conjunction with the Dove Campaign for Real Beauty, only 4 percent of women around the world consider themselves beautiful, 72 percent of girls feel tremendous pressure to be beautiful, and 80 percent of women agree that every woman has something about her that is beautiful but do not see their own beauty.[1]

There is particular pressure on girls that starts very early in life, picks up intensity in middle school, and persists well into adulthood. A major aspect of social currency for girls and women continues to be rooted in physical appearance, including clothing and accessories designed to enhance a certain look. Peers, marketing campaigns, social media, fashion magazines, and tabloids fuel the pressure on girls and women by giving them constant reminders of what they could and should look like. The primary intention of many mainstream products and marketing campaigns is to convince people that they are not enough and need the product to improve their appearance. This is further exacerbated by modern hyperconnectivity, which pushes girls and women to constantly compare themselves with others, reinforcing the notion that the way they look is somehow wrong. Rather than existing comfortably in their own skin, many women engage in what Dr. Caroline Heldman, professor of politics at Occidental College, calls "habitual body monitoring":

> What is habitual body monitoring? We think about the positioning of our legs, the positioning of our hair, where the light is falling, who's looking at us, who's not looking at us....In fact, in the five minutes that I've been giving this talk, on average, the women in this audience have engaged in habitual body monitoring ten times. That is every thirty seconds. Eating disorders are much more prevalent with those who see themselves as sex objects, as well as suffer from body shame and depressed cognitive functioning. If we're engaging in habitual body monitoring, it simply takes up more mental space that could be better used completing a math

test, completing your homework. It just sucks our cognitive functioning.[2]

Body image is an issue for boys and men as well, but they are reluctant to complain openly, often because they are expected to be emotionally unaffected and strong. Pressures surrounding body image are mainly unspoken and unacknowledged among guys who are friends. Being athletic, muscular, and well-endowed are three attributes that give boys and men more social currency, particularly among other guys. While there aren't as many products on the market directed at males, the message that you must look a certain way is conveyed through bodybuilding websites, popular video games, marketing, movies, and Internet porn.

> "Because I was constantly disappointed about how I looked in middle and high school (overweight, not muscular), I've subconsciously developed the twisted belief that physical appearance is the most important factor when it comes to overall success in life. My current bodybuilder-like physique and weightlifting habits are a result of that belief."
>
> —Male, age twenty

PROMOTING HEALTHY MASCULINITIES

Mark Tappan, Professor of Education and Human Development,
Colby College

There is much talk these days, in the popular and academic press, about the so-called "boy crisis." Primarily this is a concern about the decline in academic performance and engagement of boys and young men in elementary, middle, and high schools, as well as in colleges and universities. Concerns, however, focus also on nonacademic issues involving boys and young men, including, most significantly, the perpetration of sexual violence.

There is mounting evidence that adherence to traditional masculine norms and stereotypes (e.g., emotional stoicism, toughness, autonomy, aggression/violence) is academically, psychologically, and socially harmful, and may be responsible, at least in part, for the challenges and problems that boys and young men currently face. Some boys and young men, however, reject these traditional norms and, instead, embrace what might be called "resistant" or "healthy" forms of masculinity (e.g., expressing emotional vulnerability, valuing intimacy/interdependence, renouncing aggression/violence). Most importantly, recent research suggests that such resistance to traditional forms of masculinity leads to increased educational success, as well as to positive psychological and social outcomes.[3]

Given these promising research results, I have been working with my students at Colby College, a small liberal arts college in Waterville, Maine, to develop strategies to promote healthy forms of masculinity, and to encourage boys and young men to work for gender equity, and to prevent sexual violence. These strategies are intended to go beyond bystander intervention and other models of sexual violence prevention, to move toward primary prevention efforts that seek to challenge and change broader cultural assumptions about masculinity, male privilege, and male entitlement.

One of these initiatives entails students from my Boys to Men class, working in coed pairs, leading weekly discussion groups with elementary and middle school boys. The goal of these groups is to support the development of healthy forms of masculinity by constructing "hardiness zones" for boys,[4] that help boys to resist the most debilitating pressures of conventional masculinity, to develop a critical perspective on the culture in which they live, and to form genuine and meaningful relationships with both peers and adults.

Group leaders work with a common curriculum, which includes team building, media literacy, and social justice activities. Groups also undertake an end-of-the-semester social action project, designed to identify an issue of unfairness/injustice in their schools, and to enable boys to gain skills as activists and change agents.

Another initiative entails work with Mules Against Violence (MAV), a student organization whose mission is to work with male-identified athletes to raise awareness about the prevalence of sexual violence in the college community, as well as to challenge gender norms and stereotypes. As president of MAV, Eric Barthold ('12) developed a curriculum for facilitated conversations on masculinity, male privilege, sexual assault, and sexual health that were conducted with all of Colby's male sports teams. These conversations aim to spark peer-to-peer discussions and amplify the healthy voices within the male student–athlete population, which inherently holds a great amount of social power on campus. Since graduating from Colby in 2012, Eric has adapted these conversations, now titled *"Man Up" and Open Up* (manupandopenup.com), in order to bring them to high school and middle school groups around New England and even South Africa.

A third initiative was spearheaded by Jonathan Kalin ('14), who took over the leadership of MAV after Eric graduated. John developed the *Party With Consent* (partywithconsent.org) movement, which started with the distribution of neon tank tops emblazoned with the "Party With Consent" slogan, and quickly grew into affirmative-consent-themed memes, music, and parties, all designed to bring the discussion about consent out of the dark and into the mainstream. Another successful initiative was Date Week, a week of highly publicized discounts at local restaurants if students showed up with a date. These efforts were designed to simultaneously create space for men (and women) to think critically about the current campus culture around consent, sexual relationships, and gender dynamics, and to provide options for them to act and interact in more healthy and empowering ways.

Working with committed and courageous young men like Eric and John (and many others) is absolutely inspiring, and it makes all of the hard work worthwhile. Disrupting traditional, unhealthy forms of masculinity and replacing them with healthy masculinities is a task that is challenging, ongoing, and never ending. But it is also exciting and energizing, and it holds the potential to help us move toward a world in which justice, compassion, and mutual respect are the hallmarks of all intimate relationships.

What Is a Normal Penis Size?

Anxiety levels are high among young men about penile adequacy, including length, shape, diameter, and general appearance, as well as about whether or not they are circumcised. Men are eager to know if they fit the norm. According to many porn-consuming men, porn makes you question whether your penis is adequate. The average size of a penis in porn is more than eight inches. When a guy is repeatedly exposed to anaconda-sized penises while watching porn, he is at risk of becoming worried about his own penis. Having spoken to many heterosexual women about this issue, I can tell you that most women are relieved that you don't have an anaconda-sized penis. And if you are one of the rare fellas who does, bring a tube of lube!

• According to the *British Journal of Urology International*, approximately 85 percent of women report being "satisfied with their partners' penile size," but only 55 percent of men reported satisfaction with the size of their own penis.[5]

- The same article in the *British Journal of Urology International*, which was a meta-analysis of various studies performed on men of a variety of nationalities, ages, and sexual orientations, reported the following measurements as average for penile size across groups:

Flaccid: Length 12–13 cm (4.7–5.1 in)
Girth 9–10 cm (3.5–4 in)
Erect: Length 14–16 cm (5.5–6.3 in)
Girth 12–13 cm (4.7–5.1 in)[6]

- The average depth of a vagina when the woman is in a state of arousal is only 4.25 to 4.75 inches. Your penis is probably plenty long![7]

"My 'figuring out' was done by trial and error and looking online. When I was thirteen, I was very self-conscious about my penis size and hesitant to receive a hand job. I thought girls expected a penis to be around six inches long. On a good day, I was pushing three and a half inches at the time. Worrying about my penis size during a sexual encounter in high school led to anxiety about getting an erection."

—Male, age twenty-two

Why Do Many Young Guys Suffer from Erectile Dysfunction?

Male college students e-mail me privately about erectile dysfunction (ED) concerns more than anything else. The fact that 5 percent of men in their twenties report having ED indicates that it is more of an issue for younger men than many people think.[8] Angst around getting an erection, fumbling with a condom, antidepressant medication, obesity, drugs, and alcohol all contribute to ED in younger men.[9] While some articles and research claim there is no link between porn and ED, anecdotal evidence and studies like the one conducted by the Society of Andrology and Sexual Medicine (SIAMS), which surveyed twenty-eight thousand men, are convincing. Over the past eleven years, I have consistently heard from young men who report that their erectile dysfunction issues subsided when they quit viewing porn. These kinds of experiences are echoed in an extensive number of personal stories contributed to websites designed as resources for young men seeking support and perspective. If you want to read personal stories of young guys who have had issues with porn, you will find an overwhelming number of perspectives on the website Your Brain on Porn (yourbrainonporn.com).[10]

Dr. Tyger Latham, a Washington, D.C., psychologist, found himself convinced by personal reports from his clients, as well as accounts on dozens of websites and message boards, that ED is the result of a complicated combination of physiological and psychological factors. Reports that porn does not impact the sexual experiences of young men are not particularly convincing. Many habitual porn consumers report that taking a break from porn helped them get back on track when they struggled with sexual anxiety, including ED. The results from a study of twenty-eight thousand Italian men align with what I hear from a number of college men: researchers found "gradual but devastating" effects of repeated exposure to pornography over a long period of time. The head of the study, Carlos Forsta, reports that the problem "starts with lower reactions to porn sites, then there is a general drop in libido and in the end, it becomes impossible to get an erection."[11]

In older men, ED may be caused by underlying medical conditions such as heart disease, or can be a side effect of some medications. Among younger men, however, the causes are more often psychological. There are rare cases of what is called primary ED, in which a man has never been able to have an erection, but the majority are secondary cases, in which the man has had normal erectile function in the past but is now facing problems. The psychological causes in these cases include:

- Depression
- Stress or anxiety about a nonsexual problem
- Performance anxiety
- Relationship problems that make sex undesirable or not pleasurable

And, of course, there's the one we're all familiar with: whiskey dick, a man's inability to get an erection after consuming alcohol or another substance.

To better understand ED, let's take a quick look at the physical mechanics of erection. The penis contains "chambers" made of spongy erectile tissue, which flood with blood when a man becomes aroused. The Cornell Medical College Department of Urology explains it as follows: when a man is stimulated (whether physically or mentally), "chemicals are released in the brain that cause signals to pass down the spinal cord and outward through special nerves (nervi erigentes) into the penis. These nerves release another chemical (nitric oxide) that causes the aforementioned smooth muscle to relax and blood rushes into the erectile bodies, causing erection."[12] That is to say, an erection depends on the brain releasing certain chemicals that trigger a chain response and results in those erection chambers filling up. When a man is stressed or anxious, however, those initial brain signals get repressed, making it impossible for him to get hard. Point being, there's nothing wrong with the guy or his penis—the brain just thinks something is happening in the outside world that would make this a bad time to get an erection (ironically, it often seems to think that at just about the only time when it *would* be good to have one).

Why Do Women Go Out with Guys Who Are Dicks?

It's a perplexing situation: many women claim that they want a nice guy, but then go out with a guy who acts like a dick. I know you young people get tired of hearing adults in committed long-term relationships telling you to take the high road because it will pay off. If you interviewed a lot of happy, committed couples, you would hear stories about people who landed in excellent relationships after they grew up, figured things out, and emotionally woke up. But the short term is more your concern. What many young guys are asking is: Why are so many assholes getting laid and finding girl-friends? It is maddening, and has been for generations. There is no clear answer; the only thing you can control is how you react to the situation.

This situation—in which people seem to choose dates or sexual partners who are not worthy of them—is universal. Because you can't control whom others choose for a hookup or committed relationship, dig deep and put your energy toward yourself. By engaging in other things—your friendships, your studies, and the things you do for fun—you will avoid the obsessive irritation that this perception can create. People who spend time comparing themselves with others, obsessing about injustice, seething with envy, and feeling bitter about what they think is missing in their own lives tend to develop a vibe that can be a repellent. Bitterness can grow quickly and bring you down, and we have all witnessed the sour attitude of friends or been there ourselves. The situation can become magnified if a bitter friend reaches a certain point of intoxication and starts to vent his or her true feelings, sometimes loudly and repetitively in public. It could be the sight of a random person or the mention of a name that triggers a person to unleash anger, hurt, loneliness, and confusion.

I have noticed, as both a friend and an interviewer of many boys and men over the last decade, that the tendency toward bitterness is more common among guys, mainly because they watch so many of their female crushes or good female friends choose guys who don't treat them well. The restraint required to stay friends with these women is challenging for many guys, who complain that it is really hard to appreciate that there is something more to their friend's boyfriend; they are blinded by what they perceive or know about the guy. Hanging out with the female friend and her boyfriend is frustrating, sometimes because it makes them jealous and sometimes because they believe their friend deserves better. While plenty of women feel this way about the choices their male friends make, they are generally less engaged in trying to change the situation; the frustration and anger from individuals and groups of guys, on the other hand, tend to linger with more intensity. I hear a lot of this.

Why Are Guys Expected to Appear Unemotional?

Most parents hope to have children who are strong, independent individuals, but the next best thing is for their kids—particularly the boys—to give the outward appearance of being normal. What it takes to stay in the range of normal can wear on a boy's emotional well-being. We live in a culture that, fueled by marketing and media, celebrates and normalizes hypermasculinity. Boys rarely get support when they hit their emotional threshold or feel different, alone, shamed, or humiliated. When a boy is able to express his full range of emotions without restraint, he will be less likely to act out, feel a need to prove his worth, or elevate himself at the expense of others. With the help of recent research and personal stories of men, we are beginning to acknowledge that guys experience more emotional complexity than is often evident.

Eric Barthold, speaker and creator of the program "Man Up" and Open Up (manupandopenup.com), describes how boys of all ages define what it means to be a man in mainstream society, as well as what is not considered manly. Barthold facilitates a "man box" exercise he has adapted over the years, influenced by various masculinities experts, including Paul Kivel, one of the first to identify the way our culture perpetuates the "act like a man" requirement. Barthold draws a box and a defined area outside the box. As the group offers words that fit our cultural definition of "manly," Barthold writes them inside the box. The suggested words that describe our cultural definition of "*not* manly" are written the outside of the box. He also has a space for the overlap between the outside and inside of the "man box." Barthold explains:

> The problem with our concept of masculinity lies in the pressure that boys and men feel to be in the "man box" all the time (fitting conventional expectations of masculinity such as being physically strong, sexually confident, and cool). In reality, no guy can achieve that. And if we say that it's impossible to stay in that box, then we're saying it's impossible to live up to our society's idea of what it means to be a man. Guys will never feel "enough" in this context until they recognize the pressures of their gender and work to expand the "man box" by living both inside and outside our culture's impossibly narrow definition of a man.

After the group generates lists of words, Barthold asks each participant to describe a man in his life whom he admires and aspires to be like when he gets older; it is fascinating how most guys describe a man who possesses many of the qualities that are outside the "man box" (the men participants admire are often emotional, expressive, sensitive, caring). It seems that many boys and young men think they can eventually be like the man they admire, once they endure the common pressures on guys and ultimately prove themselves worthy of acceptance in social groups or on teams. As a culture, we have only recently started to acknowledge that the shaming, hazing, and bullying many boys endure is quite damaging. Boys are fed the idea that when they achieve a certain goal, make a team, are accepted into a specific school, get accepted into an organization, are hired for a particular job, earn a certain amount of money, or date a conventionally beautiful woman they will feel enough. The reality is that our culture is set up to have guys on the run to fit a narrow ideal. It turns out no guy will feel enough until he can genuinely let go of the criteria placed on him by society and the culture and live on his own terms.

Our assumption that guys lead uncomplicated emotional lives serves to limit their self-expression. Rosalind Wiseman, author of *Masterminds and Wingmen,* nails it: "Frankly, we find it really challenging to admit how much we contribute to boys' alienation. But make no mistake—under that detached façade, boys are desperate for meaning in their lives and for relationships they can count on for support and love."[13]

Masculinities researcher Josiah Proietti aims to give clearer emotional direction to boys and young men and help them find gender-balanced routes throughout boyhood, their teen years, and into manhood. Proietti says:

> Progressive perspectives tend to focus on the messages that boys receive about toughening up (e.g., boys don't cry, real men should be in control) yet miss the messages young men internalize about *not* toughening up (e.g., don't be a "dick," don't be a "sleaze"). Most boys and men feel a great tension between these contradictory messages. Don't be a pussy, but don't be an asshole. Nice guys finish last, but all women

really want is a sensitive man. More and more men get lost between two undesirable choices: (1) man up and suffer the feminist critique of being too masculine or (2) soften down and suffer the shame of being too feminine. We often fail to understand the impact this "no win" choice has on young male development.

Proietti describes his own experience at age five of catching sight of a man in leather driving a loud motorcycle. Just as he got excited and leaned forward to take in this classic example of masculine power, his mother sarcastically made fun of the man, expressing how deeply she disapproved of such displays of masculinity. He knows now that his mother wanted to help him avoid the pitfalls of one-dimensional masculinity, but she failed to offer him a balanced alternative. All five-year-old Josiah understood was that, although he was drawn to the man on the motorcycle, he was not supposed to be like him. He was torn between his natural interest and the expectations of his mom.

Reconciling the pressures to toughen up with those to soften up, balancing the natural drive to be tough with inherent vulnerability, is challenging. Connections with older men who are willing to share personal stories about self-doubt and overcoming emotional setbacks help reinforce that a full spectrum of emotions is healthy and normal. Proietti asserts that showing vulnerability is an act of strength, and that "being vulnerable is believing that we are lovable even with our flaws."

How Can I Stop Obsessing About My Looks?

It takes effort to break the cycle of self-criticism and the tendency to focus on your perceived inadequacies. Challenge yourself to acknowledge five things your like about your appearance every time you step up to a mirror, rather than scrutinizing what you don't like. Even if you can only appreciate your pinky finger or your elbow, it is a start.

> "Basically, every day my mind finds some area where I am inadequate in comparison to other girls. I am not sexual enough, or I am too sexual. I am too stupid, or I talk too much in class. I am ugly, or I think too highly of myself. It takes extreme effort to bring myself back to reality."
>
> —Female, age eighteen

Be mindful of the way you talk about your own appearance and that of others. Pay attention to all the ways you are marinated in reminders that you are not enough through media, marketing, social media, and peers. Moving through your life with conviction is amazingly contagious; when you spend less time obsessing about your looks and get behind the body you are in, the people around you tend follow suit. Work toward living in your body with more conviction. Own it!

It is worth discussing how cultural messaging breeds envy, insecurity, and depression. Develop a discerning eye for the messages seeking to influence you on a variety of platforms by talking about them with friends who are seeing the same things. Consider how you might feel if you reduced your exposure to magazines, TV shows and movies, advertisements, and social media. Resist commenting about who is hot and gorgeous, and resist checking for likes and comments on you own photos. Remember that people carefully cultivate their image on social media, and that it often doesn't match reality. What are ads telling you that you need to do and get to be more attractive? What would it be like to try a media and technology detox for a short period of time? Aside from the risk of being left out of the fast-moving, constant communication among your peers, how might a media detox change your frame of mind and feelings of self-worth?

It requires some fire and gusto to break the cycle of self-criticism. One way to sneak up on yourself is to look at your reflection in the mirror and find three aspects of your appearance for which you are grateful. At first, you may only appreciate your elbow, pinkie, or earlobe. Cling to that elbow like a life raft by holding it out front so you can soak up its wonders. When the doubt creeps in, step away and don't return until you are prepared to fully embrace the beauty of your pinkie. The list will grow with practice.

Why Do So Many Women Think They Need Vaginal Surgery?

Many more women have developed genital image issues, thanks to the influences of porn and a marketing-created problem (see chapter 4, "Porn"). Surgically altered labia may seem common and necessary because we see advertisements for "vaginal rejuvenation," "vaginal reconstruction," "labiaplasty," "vaginoplasty," and "vaginal cosmetic surgery" plastered across websites and the backs of magazines aimed at women consumers. The marketing alone can contribute to women's feelings of self-consciousness about their vulvas, and seeing or even hearing what women in porn look like reinforces concern about labia size and vulva appearance. Women in porn have their pubic hair removed and their vulvas surgically altered to look like those of teenagers and preteen girls because it is illegal to use underage actors in porn, and this practice creates expectations among viewers of porn. (*Vulva* refers to the visible, external genitals and *vagina* is the internal part that leads to the cervix.)

According to a study by *BJOG: An International Journal of Obstetrics and Gynaecology*, "Women vary widely in genital dimensions. This information should be made available to women when considering surgical procedures on the genitals, decisions for which must be carefully considered between surgeon and women."[14] Surgical solutions may be appropriate for a woman who has abnormally large labia that cause serious pain or discomfort, but those conditions are much more rare than marketing for labia surgeries would indicate. Most recipients of these surgeries choose to go forward because they believe their vulvas are not normal, a result of feedback from sexual partners or a lack of information about how normal female vulvas appear.

> "When I was sixteen, my boyfriend told me I should get rid of my pubic hair. He said, 'All women wax their pubic hair off.' I believed him and shaved it off. I regretted it. Then he told me I was too flappy. Soon after, I figured out that 'all women' were the women he saw in porn."
>
> —Female, age twenty-one

The takeaway for heterosexual women is this: guys probably aren't thinking all that much about how your vulva looks—they're grateful to be having sex with you. If a guy is confused about why your vulva looks different from the ones he has seen in porn, there's a decent chance that he hasn't seen too many vulvas in three dimensions. Instead of getting embarrassed, consider it an opportunity to educate him about what women really look like. Some women with female partners are getting caught up in the pressure to look different as a result of pervasive marketing campaigns and cultural expectations. For some perspective on the vast range of women's genital appearance, it is worth checking out Jamie McCartney's sculpture titled *The Great Wall of Vagina,* a large wall sculpture made up of the plaster casts of four hundred women's vulvas.[15]

Why Is There an Expectation About Removing Pubic Hair?

There has been a marked trend in recent years toward removing pubic hair, especially for women, but *manscaping* has become a normal practice for a good number of young men. When asked, many men say that removing pubic hair makes their penis look bigger. When pressed for justification, some young women claim that they wax or shave their pubic hair to give better access to their clitoris. Access to the clitoris is not usually hair related, since there is no hair on the clitoris or the clitoral hood. Back in the seventies, pride in a righteous bush of pubic hair, along with a lot of other hair, was all the rage and was part of a message that you were unrestrained by cultural expectations and norms. It was also a time when many more young women *and* men had full knowledge of the clitoris and its capacity for pleasure, a concept that was part of the conversations of sexually active young people. Unfortunately, pleasure education has been absent from open conversations among young people for the last few decades. The presence of pubic hair, however, shouldn't be an obstacle to the clitoris.

The primary motivator for removing pubic hair in this day and age is appearance. Hair is simply considered unsightly by some. Most people who remove their pubic hair are shaving rather than waxing it, because shaving costs less and doesn't require a salon visit. Waxing or shaving can cause skin irritation, rashes, ingrown hairs, and infections. As unsightly and uncomfortable as these common conditions are, many people are willing to endure them. In fact, there is a growing trend of mothers who don't want their daughters to be bothered with pubic hair taking their middle school–age girls to get rid of hair follicles before the pubic hair grows.

I rarely hear women express a preference over a male partner's pubic hair. Many heterosexual women admit they wouldn't really notice or care. Despite the feedback young women get from male partners whose ideas about pubic hair are influenced by culture, porn, and peers, most heterosexual guys will not forgo a sexual opportunity based on the presence of pubic hair. Several confident young women I know put that theory to the test and reported how quickly pubic hair became a nonfactor when they addressed the issue directly with their male partners.

Why Do Some Guys Expect Me to Act Like a Porn Star?

Most heterosexual men are not as selective as they are accused of being. More than a decade of interviews has made it clear to me that most men aren't looking for sexual partners who look and act like women in magazines or porn. "Hot" by most men's real-life standards is about a woman's genuine sexual responsiveness and comfort with her body. Men repeatedly tell me they are grateful for the opportunity to be naked with a woman. A common turnoff for men, however, is when a woman focuses on what she doesn't like about her body during sex rather than enjoying the experience. Men are often less worried about fat on their partner's thighs and more interested in getting between them (graphic, but true). Being self-conscious during sex is not only unnecessary, but can make the sexual experience worse for you; in her TED Talk, Caroline Heldman says, "Body monitoring during sex, aka 'spectatoring' during sex, interferes with sexual pleasure!"[16] So, choose your own brand of "hot" by getting behind the body you were blessed with.

Too many people enter adulthood expecting to suddenly get over their feelings of sexual and physical inadequacy. When the angst doesn't subside, people assume it is too late to ask for input. Some people tap into a vast array of resources on the Internet, which can be daunting and may cause more confusion. I am inspired to keep doing this work by the reactions I get from audiences of college students who are searching for answers, by the guys who leap from their seats for high fives after they hear about average penis size and the young women who thank me for helping them embrace their layer of "frosting" rather than fret about the pounds they think they should lose to be "worthy."

Many young men thank me privately or by e-mail for talking openly about the relentless pressure to be "man" enough. Hardly anyone has talked openly to women about the way they are under pressure to look like the women in porn. Generally, new information provides relief from feelings of inadequacy and helps people move forward with more realistic expectations. Modern media causes most of this confusion, which makes it extremely important that we take a closer look at how we are really using this resource for connection.

2

Connecting

Navigating the World of Texting, Twitter, and Tinder

The number of options and types of influences we are managing in the digital age make it challenging to understand what is really right for us. Sometimes it's hard to distinguish between what we value and what we *think* we should value based on what we see on our phones, on social media, and through online and print marketing. As a society, we have reached a point where we need to actively choose to unplug, slow down, be alone, and pay attention to one another and the world around us. Making healthy decisions requires listening to your heart, feeling what is in your gut, knowing your own mind, and following your instincts—when you do this, you are following your own inner compass, the guiding interior force that indicates the right direction for you through awareness, perspective, forethought, and reflection. Tapping into your inner compass, however, requires focus.

"That's the thing about the Internet: It doesn't simply help us find the best thing out there: it has helped to produce the idea that there *is* a best thing and, if we search hard enough, we can find it. And in turn there are a whole bunch of inferior things that we'd be foolish to choose."

—Aziz Ansari, *Modern Romance*

Acknowledging the factors that clutter our lives can help us develop the filters we need to sort through the many options, narrow our view, and prevent us from turning minor choices into a series of endless comparisons. In a *Fresh Air* interview, Dr. Frances E. Jensen, chair of the neurology department at the University of Pennsylvania Medical School and author of *The Teenage Brain: A Neuroscientist's Survival Guide to Raising Adolescents and Young Adults,* confirmed our need to examine the way we engage with information and input. Host Terry Gross asked Jensen to address the fact that people are overwhelmed by constant streams of information, yet also crave it.[1] According to Jensen, medical education started taking a different approach to learning a few decades ago. Because there are too many facts to memorize during medical school, students are being taught efficient ways "to access information rather than absorbing, digesting, and ingraining that information... [doctors] cannot possibly stay up to date by memorizing everything.... Students are developing the skill of scanning and also validating information sources and knowing where to go when."[2] As social beings in the digital age, we need to be mindful in order to identify what is important and valuable information and be able to weed out the clutter. Mindfulness requires practice.

"Being mindful," "being present," and "staying in the moment" are no longer considered way-out concepts: they are standard advice from medical doctors, therapists, counselors, and life coaches. The fact that such a large number of people suffer from physical and emotional health problems indicates that we are more unmoored than ever. Many people who are aware that their lives are out of balance have adopted meditation and yoga as daily practices. Being caught up in the treadmill of life has led people to seek more peace and harmony, search for a stronger sense of purpose, and take a step back to live in the moment. As college students, you are managing your own version of the treadmill and figuring out how to set priorities and maintain balance in your lives.

"It took me a while to discover my own heart, but the pain of being disconnected from it was overwhelming and had obvious consequences. Fortunately, I learned to meditate with excellent guidance."

—William Okin, Thacher School math teacher
and practicing Buddhist

Tuning in to one's inner compass was a much easier task before smartphones and social media dominated the social landscape. Life, choices, and relationships seemed simpler, because our access to our friends and to the wider network of acquaintances and friends' friends was more restricted. We were less aware of what was going on in the lives of people who didn't go to our school or live in our neighborhood. Neurologist and brain development expert Dr. Frances E. Jensen points out that smartphone use is clearly disrupting sleep patterns, and there is speculation that electronic distractions are changing brains. Experts wonder whether people will adapt to these disruptions, but the clearest evidence won't be in until the kids in this latest generation—who have used devices from babyhood—reach their thirties. When describing kids who spend a lot of time on devices, Jensen explains, "They are not mindful about how to manage this input."[3] Current research shows that brains continue to develop into the mid-twenties.

As a pioneer in this new age of social media and rapidly advancing technology, you need to find a healthy balance between real and virtual activities. Balancing screen time with time spent outside, reading a book, creating something, or interacting with others face to face is a worthwhile effort. Taking a break from studying, especially when it involves staring at a screen, helps reboot your energy and focus. When computers became part of daily use in the 1990s, the general advice was to spend as much time outside in nature as you did sitting in front of the screen. These days, that advice would be nearly impossible to follow because so many of our obligations and downtime activities are accessed online. On a cold or rainy weekend, time in front of a screen can unravel into hours on the couch. You might find it easy to justify eight hours of movies because that is nothing compared with the dozens of hours your friends waste watching shows and videos or playing games online.

Finding My Own Inner Compass

I was lucky enough to grow up in a household that encouraged me to discover my own inner compass. As the youngest of seven children in a device-free age, I had the opportunity to observe a lot of the choices my siblings made and the consequences of those choices, both positive and negative. Initially, my parents attempted to shield us younger ones from discipline situations and the relationship issues of the older kids, but it was impossible to contain the volume and emotional intensity of my siblings' interactions with our parents. Listening from the next room meant we only got part of the story, which was worse than the whole truth in some cases.

My parents made an executive decision to invite the youngest kids to the table of negotiation around the personal issues of our older siblings. It was a feast of learning about friendship, relationships, marriage, drug and alcohol use, academic challenges, and the consequences of choosing to abide or not abide by laws and family rules. My parents made it clear to all of us that when we did something wrong, we had to pay the consequences in order to learn and grow. They viewed failures and setbacks as learning opportunities. It became overwhelmingly clear to me that finding one's way through life was an ongoing experience of challenge and adaptation. Witnessing the outcomes of my older siblings' decisions contributed to my own development of forethought, risk assessment, personal values, and a strong inner compass. My older brothers and sisters cleared a six-lane highway for the younger siblings.

The Void

The Internet and social media relentlessly barrage us with reminders, posts, and images about other people's lives, constantly sending messages about what we could, should, or would be if we only purchased certain products, made certain choices, or engaged in certain behaviors. It is not surprising that people today experience deeper feelings of emptiness—of an internal void—than those in previous generations. Knowledge of the specific details of other people's possessions and lifestyles can set an expectation and standard for anyone who spends a lot of time online or using social media. The bar gets high pretty quickly. Intensive awareness of the many things that can be purchased, worn, seen, or done means that keeping up is a constant scramble and can distance us from our own desires and thoughts. With so much stimulation readily available on phones, tablets, and computers, we are spending less time with our own thoughts and more time filling the void with technological input of one kind or another.

Boredom was once something people endured, and spent energy and creativity to move through. Now, people reach for a device at the first sign of restlessness and in the first moment of free time. Many college professors remark on what happens at the end of class now: instead of a murmur of conversation filling the room, silence remains, as students immediately zone in on their phones. When I ask college students what it would feel like to walk to their next class or back to the dorm without looking at their phone, "lonely" is a common response. A number of students readily admit that they have pretended to be reading texts while walking alone because they feel awkward otherwise. Checking your phone catches on like yawning. When one person pulls out a phone, others pull out their own phones to see what is going on and who is in touch. FOMO (fear of missing out) is a slow-burn, pervasive social state that drives many people to keep checking their phones.

Engaging on your phone as a default and a space filler when you are sitting around with a group of friends has quickly become an acceptable habit. Sometimes people depend on the content of a text, video, or photo to start a conversation with the group. They also use the phone to pull away from but remain sitting with others. This creates the paradox of being apart and together—a new norm for people of all ages. If a couple of people in a group put their phones away, it is more likely that others will follow suit and reengage with the group. These patterns of phone use in groups seem to be accepted, and occur with little or no discussion.

"When I am sitting around talking with friends, if one person brings out his phone, everyone else pulls out their phone one by one. It has become a thoughtless habit."

—Female, age nineteen

Many of the college students I talk to are surprisingly willing to consider self-regulating their technology use. It seems that most of you agree that face-to-face interactions need to be balanced with online communication. Most also agree, though, that the efficiency of communicating through devices is hard to resist or avoid. Socializing on a screen went unchecked for years, even when dependence on phones had become standard.

Psychologist Yalda T. Uhls, author of *Media Moms and Digital Dads: A Fact-Not-Fear Approach to Parenting in the Digital Age*, conducted a study of preteens and screen time. Uhls was lead author on a 2014 study, *Computers in Human Behavior,* to determine "whether looking at screens, rather than at people, could shape learning about the social world."[4] Her team did pre- and posttests with kids who attended an outdoor camp and had no access to phones, TV, tablets, or computers and another group who attended school as usual. Uhls concluded that after five days without phones or tablets, these campers were able to correctly identify the emotions of people in photos and videos significantly better than a control group, confirming what the camp counselors had noticed in kids after just a few days at camp.[5]

The study concluded that "the short-term effects of increased opportunities for social interaction, combined with time away from screen-based media and digital communication tools, improves a preteen's understanding of nonverbal emotional cues."[6] Empathy, according to this study, is fostered by conversations in which people pay close attention to others and learn how to put themselves in someone else's shoes.[7] The upside of this study is that the damage to social skills is reversible for preteens if appropriate intervention is offered. For adults—who have fully developed brains, as well as work, social, and family responsibilities calling relentlessly through screens—how will the damage to social skills manifest if screen time is left unchecked?

Screen Time and Social Media

Thirty years ago, young people felt pretty special if a handful of peers considered them to be mildly interesting and called them on the phone occasionally. The pressure to be wildly interesting to hundreds of people on a daily basis in multiple public forums is exhausting, and it is taking an emotional toll. Poring over other people's photos and posts can lead to feelings of inadequacy, jealousy, and resentment. Social media platforms give users the opportunity to put their best face forward—and in some cases it's a completely false image. It is important to remember that the people whose lives we admire through social media have often spent hours editing their photos and posts to create an impression of perfection that does not reflect reality. College students report that viewing their friends' feeds, with flattering photos and posts about their exciting lives and the fabulous places they visit, makes them feel boring, uninteresting, and pathetic sitting in their dorm room in their sweatpants. People also feel left out when they see posts about parties, events, or gatherings to which they were not invited. It is easy to get caught up in viewing for hours, reinforcing the warped perception that everyone else's lives are more interesting than your own.

The truth is that humans are complicated and multidimensional, and have the capacity to be excellent people with flaws and also be physically attractive with bad days. Social media, however, isn't the venue in which our multidimensional selves, including our misgivings, foibles, and literal and figurative pimples, are presented.

Multitasking

Multitasking is the term people use to justify flying from task to task and device to device. People of all ages claim to be multitaskers. In a 2013 interview on NPR's *Talk of the Nation*, Clifford Nass, psychology professor at Stanford, said, "High multitaskers think of themselves as great at multitasking."[8] Research shows, however, that multitasking trains the brain to be more susceptible to distraction and causes the multitasker to lose the ability to focus. According to Nass's research, people who consider themselves "good at multitasking" are actually worse at it than those who are low multitaskers. The research offers a note of caution regarding the modern trend of kids navigating multiple devices from an early age.

It is common for college students to sit down to write a paper on a computer or tablet with their phone on and multiple tabs open to homework, e-mail, YouTube, or social media sites. As students attempt to write papers, they are also chatting online, reading and replying to texts, checking e-mails that pop up, seeing notifications from various social media and dealing with distracting ads in banners and sidebars on their screens. For many, the temptation to engage continuously is difficult to resist. Yet most researchers agree that multitasking is not effective. Travis Bradberry, a psychologist and *Forbes* magazine contributor, summarized current research on the topic by saying, "Multitasking reduces your efficiency and performance because your brain can only focus on one thing at a time. When you try to do two things at once, your brain lacks the capacity to perform both tasks successfully."[9]

Not only is multitasking an unproductive way to work, it also reinforces the tendency to be scattered in general. The implications for connection with others on social and sexual levels are unsettling. Take note of the way you and your peers interact. It is hard to ignore the fact that people struggle to listen to someone else complete a thought without looking at their phone, talking over the person, or losing interest in the conversation, as they drift off or start a new topic. This general lack of social patience is one result of the prevalence of one-sided communication—texting, tweeting, and posting.

Multitasking to avoid missing out is leading to shorter attention spans. Think of how often you are gathered with friends but are actually connected to and engaged with a number of people who aren't present; it is easy to get in the habit of being at a distance together. Friends spend a lot of time texting to make a plan to get together and then they sit next to each other looking at their phones, interacting with other people who are not there.

According to clinical psychologist Catherine Steiner-Adair, author of *The Big Disconnect,* young people "typically multitask on a computer, simultaneously instant messaging (IM), uploading You-Tube videos, posting updates on Facebook, and continually search-ing the Web for fresh diversions. The so-called downtime they spend on computers is neurologically, psychologically, and often emotion-ally action packed. Stimulation, hyper-connectivity, and interactiv-ity are, as the psychiatrist and creativity expert Gene Cohen put it, 'like chocolate to the brain.' We crave it."[10] It is not easy to resist the temptation to stay in constant contact and check responses.

Texting

Actor and comedian Aziz Ansari teamed up with NYU sociologist Eric Klinenberg to design a massive research project that looked at the way finding romance has evolved over the years and how the digital age has impacted the search for a partner. The results are explained in the book *Modern Romance*, in which Ansari sum-marizes the social laziness that is becoming more accepted: "As a medium, it's safe to say texting facilitates flakiness and rudeness and many other personality traits that would not be expressed in a phone call or an in-person interaction."[11]

Texting is how the bulk of communication is happening for peo-ple of college age—they make plans, check in, and pass information with great frequency and at high speed. But texts, even when emo-jis and capital letters are used, fail to convey nuance, limiting the reliability of texting as a form of communication. Students tell me they avoid calling friends on the phone because they think having a conversation would be "awkward." Reading social cues becomes increasingly challenging when you communicate on screens most of the time. It is becoming more common and acceptable for people to break up with someone through text or to hook up after communi-cating only virtually. We have come to accept, as a society, that we will use these impersonal means to talk about personal issues and feelings.

Relationships of all kinds require people to read social cues by engaging with, listening to, and observing others, because we all communicate subtly through voice tone, eye contact, body language, and facial expressions. Beginning at a young age and continuing into adulthood, people need to practice reading these cues and learning to negotiate disagreements and personal boundaries.

Ansari's personal experiences, combined with the overwhelming responses fans have to his comedy, led him to write *Modern Romance*. He interviewed a wide spectrum of individuals, from those who have been in relationships for sixty years to those who are hooking up on Tinder. Based on his research, he concludes that "younger people are so used to text-based communication, where they have time to gather their thoughts and precisely plan what they are going to say, that they are losing their ability to have spontaneous conversations."[12] People who claim they don't have time for conversations get out of practice, and often admit that they fear sounding stupid and being vulnerable. Sherry Turkle, author of *Reclaiming Conversation: The Power of Talk in a Digital Age,* explains: "The anxiety about spontaneity and the desire to manage our time means that certain conversations tend to fall away. Most endangered: the kind in which you listen intently to another person and expect that he or she is listening to you; where a discussion can go off on a tangent and circle back; where something unexpected can be discovered about a person or an idea."[13]

In addition to social skills, social courage is diminished when people depend on texts, posts, and e-mails to communicate. The sender does not have to take full responsibility for the reaction of the recipient because she does not witness it. If the recipient is hurt by a message or takes issue with it, she can also respond with a text, and thereby avoid addressing how the message impacted her. In many cases, the recipient may feel hurt and want to think about her response; she may plan to tell the sender how she felt the next time they run into each other. Because interactions are fast paced and topics shift quickly, it can be truly awkward to confront the person later because everyone has moved on. Strong connections with other people and honest conversations about emotions may become casualties of the short attention spans that are the product of fast-moving virtual interactions.

Catherine Steiner-Adair makes the point that, in terms of content, texting for young people today is similar to meeting at the park for people of previous generations. She notes that the lack of depth in texts is similar to the lack of depth in the conversation of a group of kids hanging out at a park. Aziz Ansari noted that many of the women he interviewed were annoyed by the number of guys who text them and can't seem to get beyond, "Heyyyy!" or "Whatsup?" or "Want to hang out?" Some people who keep their texts brief claim it is a way to avoid making things complicated or fear they may say the wrong thing.

In other cases, drama and stress swirl as an admirer words a text to a potential partner and finally presses send. In the introduction to his book, Ansari talks about how he had felt confident sending a carefully worded text asking a woman on a date. He became consumed by regret over what he had thought was a great text as he waited for a response that never came. This story resonates with his audiences because social lives are increasingly phone centered. It is all too common for people to experience such regret and stress, checking their phones constantly and wasting a lot of brain space figuring out how the situation could, should, or would have been different had they spent even more time crafting their texts.

Texters complain about the stress of deciding when to respond; if they reply too quickly they might seem overeager, and they want to be reassured that the tone, timing, and content of their own texts are okay. This timing game is contingent on the assumption that everyone has his phone in hand at all times (which is not an unreasonable expectation, even for people who work full time). When replies come quickly, you take that assumption for granted. When no little gray bubbles show someone is writing back and no text appears, you find ways to justify the silence by clinging to unlikely scenarios: perhaps the person dropped his phone in the toilet or forgot it somewhere. People forget their wallets and backpacks all over the place, but even the most drifty people tend to hang on to their phones.

Another downside of being caught in the comfort of "text world" is that it can be hard to break out and actually meet the person with whom you are engaging in text banter. And when you decide to meet in person, the next level of second-guessing and games begins. If you don't have strong interpersonal skills, the anticipation of awkward conversation can deter you from setting up an in-person encounter at all.

People who frequently spend their socializing time on a screen have less practice interacting face to face, and they miss opportunities to develop strong social skills. Noticing subtle shifts in body language, facial expression, and vocal tone is essential to effective communication, and it takes practice. Reading cues is particularly important in sexual situations. If people are missing cues on Tuesday afternoon in broad daylight, how can we possibly expect to pick them up in the dark, in a state of optimistic arousal, and possibly under the influence of alcohol?

Dating Apps

The use of dating apps is rising rapidly among college students, and I have interviewed people who use dating apps to arrange hookups or to set up dates. Some college students are creating their own apps for students on their campus or for students from a select group of colleges. Dating apps such as Tinder, Grindr, OKCupid, Hinge, SoulSwipe, and Match.com appeal to a variety of people, and have features that meet the interests and intentions of their users. Some are geared toward hooking up, some are geared toward dating, and some are used for both.

Dating apps have been popular among gay men since at least 2007, long before they gained the popularity they have today. In February 2015, four thousand gay men filled out an online survey from GrabHim.net that asked the question, "How Do Gay Men Act on an App?"[14] Grindr was the most popular app choice, with 29 percent of those surveyed using it, followed by Scruff (16 percent) and Tinder (10 percent). The results indicated that 31 percent of users lie about their age, height, and weight; contrary to assumptions, 45 percent of those who meet on dating apps don't hook up; 50 percent meet at their home; 30 percent don't need to see a face; and 83 percent have sent a dick pic.[15]

There is little denial among gay men that Grindr is often about hooking up, including among the men who are avid users of the app. Many heterosexual women are encouraged by their friends to use dating apps. According to one female college student, "My gay guy friends talk about dating apps much more than women. Generally, Grindr is perceived as something better for hookups and Tinder is more about relationships for gay men. I know gay couples who entered serious relationships through dating apps." This idea has been confirmed in conversations I have had with gay men ranging in age from twenty to forty.

Cindy's Take

The frequency with which women receive dick pics indicates that some fellas possess uncanny optimism. Short-term social credibility among guys may accrue for those who send such pics, but the idea that sending a dick pic will result in sexual attention from women mystifies most recipients. Some guys hope that women may keep stashes of dick pics on their computers or phones the way some guys have files of nudes and tit pics. A word from the ladies: stashes of dick pics are not a thing.

Tinder is particularly popular among heterosexual women because it eliminated the creep factor of other apps by narrowing the people who can contact you to mutual matches. Most dating apps armed creepy guys with tools to reach more women, which kept new apps from gaining purchase in the online dating world because most women deal with such guys on screen and in person on a regular basis; the false sense of courage and blind optimism some guys feel when hiding behind a screen encourages them to send off dick pics and crude texts. With Tinder, however, both people must show interest in the other by swiping right on the person's profile. This doesn't eliminate all the sketchy guys, of course. Stringing multiple people along by engaging them in Tinder text banter until they find their best option is standard practice for many.

One young woman in her mid-twenties is reconsidering Tinder: "There are some foul human beings trolling Tinder—it is a bit of a war zone out there. I did three dates on Tinder—all were pretty normal, but there was clearly a lower expectation because the meeting originated on Tinder." She had been going back and forth with a guy she thought was great, but he turned out to be a guy doing a great job of *seeming* great. When he didn't respond to her, clearly casting a wide net to many women in his search for weekend plans, she had an epiphany:

This one guy treated me as less legit because I was a Tinder find. He was pretty cool, interesting, and had a *great* sense of humor. We had mutual friends and common interests, but he was disrespectful. I wasn't having that, so he was sassed right out of my life. Tinder dates often say, 'Wow, I'm really surprised to have met someone like you on Tinder' (meaning normal and cool) as if they were only on Tinder for lower-level women they could treat like shit. If we met on Hinge or another dating app, would it have worked out because I would be considered cool and respectable?

Some people join Tinder to have fun without truly engaging. Some still consider Tinder to be more of a sleazy hookup app and think of Hinge as an app for people looking for something with a little more emotion attached. At the same time, Tinder is gaining popularity and being used for dating *and* hookups by an increasing number of women. When I ask groups of college women how many are on Tinder, about half usually raise their hands, though a smaller number have actually used it. Some women said they would consider being active on Tinder once they'd seen how the experience went for other people. Several said they had considered using it while abroad, but felt nervous in an unfamiliar place where they didn't speak the language, and where they didn't know people who could help them out if they got into a sketchy situation.

There is enough going on in the dating app world that women are careful. One Stanford student said, "I think there's still a pretty big stigma around these apps among women at Stanford. When I was in D.C. my gay guy friend was talking about how popular they are in cities and how we should all get them. The women were superhesitant to both get the apps and then actually go meet up with people from it. In a bubble-type environment, the likelihood of running into someone is really high." Plenty of people admit that checking out their matches on Tinder is an ego boost as well as an easy way to sniff out the kind of people who are out there. Some get on Tinder to entertain themselves when they are bored.

Women receive notifications from significantly more potential dates than men. Sometimes the number is so overwhelming that they can't even look at all the options. Female Tinder users often make the point that the app was originally developed by young men and was intended to help guys with their dating and sex lives. One woman in her mid-twenties in the Bay Area warns, "All of the Tinder conversations occur within Tinder until someone hands over their phone number. Then it usually moves over to text message. If you want to see the worst of the Tinder banter, check out Tinder nightmares on Instagram—horrible stuff!"

Reports from women I have interviewed confirm Ansari's observations in *Modern Romance*; a guy who would have no game in a face-to-face conversation with an attractive woman gets an inflated sense of confidence and a lot of swagger when swiping on his phone. Ansari was amazed by the regular guys swiping left after a quick view of an attractive woman's profile, claiming she wasn't quite up to snuff for one insignificant reason or another. It is notable that many of these overly confident left-swipers would never have the chance to be rejected by most of these women without dating apps, because they wouldn't muster the courage to speak to them in a bar. Making connections to hook up or go on a date is now a whole new game.

More and more people argue that swiping through dating apps is similar to deciding which person you would talk to at a bar or a party. The first moments of seeing a person from afar and the first view of a profile picture are both superficial ways to judge someone—but the interaction that immediately follows can differ greatly. When you walk into a bar or a party, you can observe the way a person interacts with others and get a sense of his or her personality by watching and listening, rather than judging the person based on basic info and a carefully chosen photo. Initiating face-to-face conversations requires you to think on your feet and possibly fumble through some awkwardness rather than learning about the other person's general interests by reading a short profile, viewing Instagram photos, checking out Facebook likes, and exchanging carefully crafted texts. Ultimately, people will have to enter a live interaction without the support of technology even if they just want to hook up.

Apps like Tinder were created to make dating simpler, yet they also make dating life stressful. Students tell me that they are caught in a double bind, wanting to match with students on campus for dating opportunities and yet being terrified of getting those matches because of the potential for awkwardness, not to mention the stress brought by mixed expectations surrounding the actual Tinder date! This is another example where interactions behind a screen don't convert to smooth interactions face to face. If you are using dating apps, muster your courage and go on actual dates, where you can work through any awkwardness and figure out if you actually match enough to go on another date. That is why "dating" apps were created.

Yik Yak Plus

Several apps, such as Yik Yak, make it possible to post abusive or hurtful comments anonymously and without consequences, and these platforms are causing problems in colleges across the country. Plenty of the banter is harmless, but it is not uncommon for funny posts to be taken too far and become malicious. While there are examples of people using different social media platforms to be cruel, anonymous posting via Yik Yak seems to bring users to a level of harassing behavior they would never have the courage to exhibit in person, even as it enables them to maintain emotional distance from their targets.

These types of platforms have led to an increase in anonymous harassment, accusations of rape and abuse, bomb threats, bullying, and racist and homophobic comments targeted at specific people on campuses. The allegations of rape and abuse, as well as the bomb threats, are easier for colleges to address than the cruelty and prejudice that undermine the sense of community. Anonymity inspires users to unleash outrageously harsh posts and follow-up comments.

Boston College Addresses Anonymous Posting

The frequency of racist yaks at Boston College inspired the FACES Council—a committee dedicated to promoting appreciation of diversity at BC—to create a video to demonstrate the harmful effects of Yik Yak on campus.[16] The video shows a series of students reading anonymous racist, sexist, homophobic, or disrespectful posts on their phones. After each person finishes, he or she looks directly at the camera for a silent moment to let the harshness of the yak sink in. The narrator ends by explaining, "Comments like these are the reason there are students at BC who are struggling to balance two cultures, struggling to maintain positive body image, and struggling to be comfortable with who they are. Yik Yak should be a red flag to the administration that there is a serious problem in the way students are being engaged in conversations about difference of race, sexual orientation, socioeconomic status, gender, and ability."[17]

The comments that follow the video online and in an accompanying letter to the editor of *The Heights*, an independent student newspaper of Boston College, reveal a surprising mix of support for the message as well as dismissal and mockery of the message. Some students suggested that people who find comments offensive should stay off Yik Yak. Others made the point that Yik Yak is just one of many platforms used to express racist attitudes, and the racist yaks reveal that the campus is in need of more conversations about intolerance and bigotry. This situation is far from unique to Boston College; the debate is going on in varying degrees on campuses everywhere, resulting in important conversations about respect and tolerance, as well as about freedom of speech and the responsibilities of different types of speech. It is my hope that students on other campuses take action to raise awareness as effectively.

Social consequences accrue when you decide to spend less time engaging with people through texts, social media, and dating apps. Friends move on to other friends when you don't respond to texts immediately. They continue a group conversation and make plans without you if you don't respond regularly. If you don't give friends a heads-up when you choose to disengage, they may worry to the point of actually coming to find you to make sure everything is okay. If you don't comment or "like" people's posts, photos, or tweets, you may feel socially irrelevant as your friends forge ahead in the online world without you. If checking matches on dating apps makes you feel noticed and attractive, you will need to adjust. For all these reasons, it takes courage to pull back from social media and text conversations with friends. If you do so, however, you will benefit from better self-awareness regarding your need to stay connected. Most people think paying too much attention to social media and checking texts causes stress, but they readily admit they can't help themselves.

When groups of friends commit to observing or curbing their own habits, they are usually willing to turn their phones off and stack them on a shelf away from the conversation. People who openly discuss online behaviors that frustrate them are more likely to pause before they share, send, or post. Letting go of the need to feel socially relevant and finding comfort in being significantly insignificant can lead to a more realistic and healthy outlook on your social life. Slowing down and paying attention to the ways you engage with your devices is a great start.

3

Unplugging

Relating to Something Other Than Your Phone

When I was fifteen, I confessed to my mother that for the ten years she required me to attend church, I never paid attention to what the priest was talking about. Without hesitation, she responded, "That may be true, but you were also not watching TV, talking, playing, or running around. You were sitting still and in your own mind for an hour a week." Touché. There are fewer and fewer opportunities for us to be in our own minds for a stretch of time before our devices beckon us to engage. Author and psychotherapist Gunilla Norris teaches meditation and leads contemplative workshops, and summarizes the need to be in our own minds in this way: "Within each of us, there is a silence, a silence as vast as the universe. And when we experience that silence, we remember who we are."[1] We have a choice to stay unplugged when we are alone. We need to remind one another and ourselves to make that choice.

Unplugging from devices, action, outside influences, media, marketing, and obligations is important for people of all ages. Being able to hear your inner compass requires you to slow down and step away from the frenzy of pressures life serves up. With the added intensity of input that comes with living in the digital age, people of all ages need to actively seek opportunities to bring their pulses down and keep their lives balanced.

You don't have to give up your phone. But if you understand its profound effects on you, you can approach your phone with greater intention and choose to live life differently with it".[2]

—Sherry Turkle author of *Reclaiming Conversation:*
The Power of Talk in a Digital Age

Self-Regulating Screen Time

By unplugging and avoiding the trap of constant digital multitasking, we give ourselves the opportunity to listen to our inner compass, our own guiding force. When you are faced with a life decision, major or minor, it is common to feel hesitant and uncertain because you are so overwhelmed. Figuring out what to study, where to live, which job to take, or what interests are worth pursuing can seem like impossible tasks because the stakes appear so high. Even when parents, advisors, coaches, and professors don't place expectations on you, you may feel intense pressure because you are overly aware of the many options available, making it hard to focus on what you really want or what feels right. Blocking out the noise around you—in both your immediate and your virtual environments—is difficult. With awareness and practice, however, you can improve your focus, become more relaxed, and find greater happiness.

The ultimate goal is to self-regulate what you consume from the culture and to work toward a healthy balance between screen time and other activities. Developing healthy values around sex, screen time, alcohol and drugs, friendship, and relationships of all kinds requires that you stay aware of the effect the invisible online world has on you. In her book *American Girls: Social Media and the Secret Lives of Teenagers,* Nancy Jo Sales summarizes girls' observations about their online lives: "There were no rules for how to behave in this new social media landscape, no guide for them to know how to respond to the way others were behaving and treating them. They were social media pioneers, but it was as if they were commanding their covered wagons without any maps or sextants."[3] People of all ages express serious concern about the time suck and distractions of our fast-moving digital world. I find it particularly interesting to watch a person glancing at her phone while making a fierce statement about how much time people waste looking at screens. Somehow, we all think we are the exception or believe that no one will mind if we check just one more time. We are self-policing our time on our phones, and we aren't very good at it. Self-regulating requires conscious consideration of the content, tone, and context of your online interactions, as well as observing how much time you spend online.

Cindy's Take

In my presentations, I make the point that everyone can access porn on their phones these days. I thought it was a fluke the first time two boys found me after my talk to tell me they had made a conscious choice to rebel against smartphones. They pulled out their old-school flip phones and beamed with pride as they noted that accessing porn on a flip phone is impossible. Because texts are a hassle on a flip phone, they use the phone to actually call and talk to people. It is becoming more common to hear about rebels in our midst who have forsaken dependence on smartphones.

Under Pressure

The documentary film *The Race to Nowhere: The Dark Side of America's Achievement Culture,* which explores the relentless pressure on kids to "succeed," resonates with parents and young people across the country, yet the race goes on. According to the film's website, "Through the testimony of educators, parents and education experts, [the film] reveals an education system in which cheating has become commonplace; students have become disengaged; stress-related illness, depression and burnout are rampant; and young people arrive at college and the workplace unprepared and uninspired."[4] In addition to this film, a multitude of articles, books, blogs posts, and news stories report that young people feel overwhelmed by expectations surrounding academic, social, and personal achievement.

Perhaps your parents feel compelled to overbook you, pushing you to build your résumé for college applications and increase your chances of getting into a "reach school"—or perhaps your parents are more laid back but you've seen your friends' parents push them. A solid number of parents stay overly involved by helping their kids with their studies, contacting professors and coaches, and even engaging in the graduate school application process. Counselors and therapists struggle to help parents recognize their inclination to push their kids and their tendency to overlook red flag behaviors associated with anxiety and stress, such as cheating, disordered eating, cutting, depression, or suicidal tendencies.

Parents may feel intense pressure to have kids who are exceptional, and this can cause some to lose perspective on what will help their children become happy, productive members of society. Remember that much of the research shows that people who are well-rounded and within the range of average are often happier than those who are driven to be exceptional. There are many other ways to lead a joyful life and make positive contributions than to become a power broker or a leader of industry.

The Emotional Cost

A number of studies indicate that many young people are depressed, overwhelmed, stressed out, and troubled by feelings of inadequacy. A common response is to try to fill the void with new stuff, such as the latest phone or tablet, another pair of expensive boots, more video games, or new clothes. The buzz of new stuff is short-lived, but the burst of elation it brings at first gives a false sense of happiness and can inspire cravings for more. Filling voids with stuff does not build lasting connection or genuine happiness, however. Roko Belic, director of the documentary film *Happy,* says, "One of the leading researchers of happiness in the world, Ed Diener, told me that a person's values are among the best predictors of their happiness. People who value money, power, fame and good looks are less likely to be happy."[5]

Overwhelming Choices

Finding balance requires that we pay attention to what distracts us. An array of choices is a luxury, but if we have too many options, life can feel overwhelming. Exploring the Internet, for example, can consume hours of your time as you look at the many options for TV shows and movies, airline tickets, ideas for ways to complete a task, resources for a project, or items to buy. Shopping online involves weighing a lot of factors before making a purchase, but shopping in a brick-and-mortar store can also be daunting.

Think about the variety of apples available in stores these days. Back in the day, we could buy a McIntosh or a Red Delicious apple, with the occasional Granny Smith showing up for a few weeks a year. These days, grocery stores have a book in the produce department that guides customers in choosing and using the many apple varieties available. I had to take a rest on the floor at Kohl's because choosing underwear for my eleven-year-old daughter was so exhausting. After we decided on the brand, we had to evaluate and find sizes, colors, and styles among the many options; there were about five styles, ranging from the granny panty to a thong trainer. At first, I had to take a knee and remove my coat; ultimately, I had a little lie down. After a nap, my daughter and I regrouped and managed to narrow our choices. With all the decisions young people have to make about their future, as well as the plan for the day in front of them, selecting apples or underwear from a vast panoply only adds to their subconscious clutter. The Internet has expanded the possibilities for everything we want, need, or think we need, but it also drains our energy, time, and brain space.

Relaxation and Meditation

I was a student athlete in the 1970s and 1980s, so it was probably inevitable that I would have a hippie as a coach somewhere along the line. Yoga's current ubiquity makes this hard to believe, but yoga was not even close to commonplace at that time. Friends and parents who happened to drive by the field where the ski team worked out had plenty of comments about our yoga poses and the guided meditation led by our high school coach. We mocked the yoga, cringed as passing cars beeped their horns at us, and shook our heads about what a waste of time it was. Our coach was a man ahead of his time, and as he had us stretch thoroughly, he asked us to intentionally slow down and pay attention to our bodies. As a ski racer in college, I reached a point at which it was necessary for me to incorporate mindfulness in order to stay focused, and I found myself conjuring up the exercises and wisdom from my old coach. It likely won't be long before mindfulness and breath work are incorporated into family life and school curricula to help kids manage all the input and counter the pressure of keeping up with the hustle of life.

Clinical social worker and therapist Lisa M. Schab, who has written books to help people of all ages find healthy inner anchors, suggests incorporating mindfulness techniques and practices into everyday life because we all need help managing stress more than ever. She explains:

> While everyone experiences anxiety, some of us feel it more often, some more deeply, some less frequently, and some less intensely. Your own experience will depend on: Genetics—how your parents, grandparents, and ancestors experienced anxiety; Brain chemistry—the type, amount, and movement of the chemicals working in your brain; Life events—the situations you are faced with in your life; and personality—how you look at and interpret things that happen to you.[6]

Schab goes on to emphasize that your "personality, or the way you perceive and handle life events, is something you have a great deal of control over—probably more than you realize." With self-awareness about our own personalities, we can adjust and develop strategies to compensate for tendencies that create stress in our lives.

As a high-strung, impulsive person, driving in traffic or bad weather causes me to be on edge and hyper-reactive. Since my kids were little, I would turn the car radio off and ask them to quiet down for a bit until we got through traffic or I could get into a groove driving in the weather. Because I openly admitted that my personality limited me in certain situations, they responded with understanding and complied with my requests. They witnessed and now remind me of strategies that help me work around the common snags in my life, including deep breathing and relaxation. Over the years, my children have become aware of their own traits and are developing strategies and relaxation techniques that work for them. Being exposed to meditation and mindfulness exercises from a young age has given them more techniques to manage stress and anxiety on their own. Meditation helps us understand ourselves better, and it lets us tap into our inner compass.

Social Courage

Social courage sets you free from pressures brought by peers, parents, and the surrounding culture. It means being comfortable with missing out—and it takes a lot of practice in a lot of different ways. Practicing nonconformity is a great way to rehearse being socially courageous. By making your own choices and establishing boundaries, you can show your close friends and peers that you are not impressionable or easily persuaded. Your college experience will be easier, and you will feel free rather than constricted once you recognize that you are not obliged to follow the agendas of others. Spending more time doing your own thing, being comfortable saying no, contradicting peers who use their social power in negative ways, and refusing to give in to social pressures can help liberate you from the expectations of others. The practice you put into doing these things fuels more courage, making you braver in situations where there is more at stake.

Most people learn to stop caring about the opinions of the crowd eventually, but some are at the mercy of others' opinions deep into adulthood. Until you make a conscious choice to disengage, it can feel like middle school never ends. Many people assume that peer pressure will simply stop when they become adults. From the land of middle age, I want you to know that there are plenty of seventh-graders-at-heart still hanging around, worried about the same old stuff. It is up to you to pull away from the attachment to what other people think.

By the time you reach college, you will most likely have taken part in bystander intervention training. These programs are designed to give you the strategies and skills you need to stand up to sexual assault, bullying, hazing, homophobia, racism, and cruelty. Administrators, parents, and other adults tend to be exasperated by students who don't muster the strength to call their peers out. In reality, the fear of social rejection or other consequences can be overwhelming, and we all need practice speaking up on small issues (litter, disrespectful language, meanness, intimidation) in order to develop the courage to stand up when the stakes are higher (sexual assault, hazing, DUI). Developing courage starts with establishing clear boundaries, feeling comfortable being your own person, and speaking up when you see others behaving unkindly.

Avoiding stress can be a daily challenge, particularly with the relentless cultural messages both online and off. Many people are concerned about their frequent consumption of media and the fact that we have collectively done so little to reflect on our constant connection to devices, but it is also easy to justify these habits as a necessary evil of the modern age. We all keep aiming to get closure, in the hope of creating space and time for something else, but closure rarely occurs. Awareness of the pressure to stay connected is the first step, but disengaging requires a conscious commitment to shifting your lens to view the many different kinds of input you are managing throughout your day. It is worth making yourself slow down, evaluate the way you engage with your devices, and reflect on how you can connect with others in a more meaningful way.

4

Porn

*How Pornography Impacts Your (Real-Life)
Sexual Relationships*

Most of you had full access to the Internet during your teenage years, and therefore many of you got a solid dose of porn directly or heard a lot about it from friends. According to current studies, the average age at which boys first view porn is eleven in the United States.[1] Recent anecdotal reports from parents, pediatricians, and sexuality educators indicate that this average seems to be getting closer to age nine. For many of you fellas, porn was your primary sexuality educator during adolescence. During the stretch of time when there wasn't much reflection about porn, your parents probably felt it wasn't their business to embarrass you with conversations about your masturbation habits, and they respected your privacy. It was probably quite easy for you to convince them that nothing was going on simply by telling them what they wanted to hear, relying on their relative technological incompetence, or making excuses for what they saw in your browsing history.

If you are like most young men, you may have made it through adolescence without having any serious conversations about masturbation or the images you were seeing in porn. This effort on the part of your parents and educators to respect your private masturbation habits, however, meant that you were exposed from a very young age to an onslaught of messaging about sex without any values-based guidance about how to interpret or understand it.

> "Thirty percent of all the data transferred across the Internet is porn. Internet porn sites get more visitors each month than Netflix, Amazon and Twitter combined."
>
> —*The Huffington Post*, May 4, 2013

Before I started conducting research and interviews about porn consumption, I assumed that Internet porn represented a harmless improvement of print porn, and that young men were getting all the answers they needed online. After the first few Q&A sessions with groups of college students, however, it was apparent that porn not only provides fantasy fuel but also serves as a sexual guide for many of you, causing confusion rather than clarifying what sex looks like and how bodies respond. Reconciling the images in porn with real-life partner experiences is challenging—it just doesn't convert. We are living in the misinformation age rather than the information age, and those who get their information about sex through porn actually know little about true pleasure.

College guys describe the increase in their online porn habit as the result of living on their own, more dependable Internet access, and stretches of time alone when their roommates are out. When I first spoke to fraternities, teams, or other all-male college groups about porn use, I was surprised by how open they were. I was enlightened to a pattern of heavy porn use among guys who were lacking a lot of key sexual knowledge, despite having plenty of sexual experience. My conversations with them offered me an opportunity to relieve the angst of at least the heterosexual men by providing them with accurate information about what their female peers were saying they did and didn't enjoy about sex (more on that in chapter 5, "Better Sex").

"Porn played a big role in influencing my ideas and expectations about sex. I thought girls liked going from slow to fast (aka the jackrabbit). Watching porn made me think anything could be a hint that a girl wanted to have sex. I also thought that every girl had a bleached asshole and shaved pubic hair. This was not the case. I have learned to always ask if it's okay with your partner before trying new things. Porn doesn't teach about how to get consent."

—Male, age twenty

Brains Wired by Porn

Distorted images and misinformation are inhibiting healthy sexual relationships. Young men readily admit they seek confirmation and clarification about what they see in porn in their real-life sexual encounters. I hear the same things time and again: frustrations, warped expectations, feelings of being misled, fear of partners faking orgasms without them knowing, and general confusion about sex and relationships. Porn seems to be magnifying feelings of inadequacy. According to Alexandra Katehakis, founder and clinical director of the Center for Healthy Sex, "When an adolescent boy compulsively views pornography, his brain chemistry can become shaped around the attitudes and situations that he is watching. Sadly, pornography paints an unrealistic picture of sexuality and relationships that can create an expectation for real-life experiences that will never be fulfilled."[2]

Men who got in the habit of using porn when they were young often hope (even assume) that masturbation and porn won't be necessary once they start "having sex all the time." Not many young men plan for a life of porn use. Instead, they optimistically view porn as a temporary gig to get them through to the promised land of regular sex with a partner. In one of my earliest interviews, a college guy naively said he would stop looking at porn and masturbating once he found a girlfriend or a wife. I had to break the news to him that in reality, masturbation would be a lifelong practice. For both men and women, it contributes to maintaining sexual health, getting through dry spells, and augmenting a healthy sex life with a partner. In spite of its importance for the sexual health of most people, however, masturbation is much more widely expected, accepted, and encouraged among guys. Evolution requires males to keep their sperm fresh, making masturbation difficult for them to avoid.

Masturbation fuel, however, has changed over the years. Some middle-aged heterosexual men react defensively to criticism of porn, assuming the critiques to be antisex and antimasturbation; these men recall their own teen encounters with *Playboy, Penthouse,* and *Hustler* with feelings of guarded nostalgia. These days, *Hustler,* once considered raunchy, feels like a greeting card compared with what is easily accessible on the Internet. Magazines are, comparatively, quite tame.

Cindy's Take

For some guys, it seems that I am the first person to alert them that masturbation occurred before the Internet was invented. The first time a guy asked me how it is possible to masturbate without porn, I expected all the other guys to give him at least a little bit of grief. Instead, the room was silent as all the guys eagerly waited for my answer. I pointed out that masturbation had been fueled by imagination since the beginning of time. The slow dawn of realization that crossed their faces begs the question: Where have all the imaginations gone?

Masturbation is all about fantasy, and online porn provides viewers with high-impact video images that they can watch conveniently and privately while avoiding emotional and physical vulnerability, risk of rejection, and shame. In fact, emotional safety is a contributing factor in the development of a porn-viewing habit among many boys and a smaller number of girls.

In my interviews, gay men have expressed much less concern, in general, about the impact of porn on their relationships. The casual shrugs and unself-conscious laughter in response to questions about porn use among gay men of all ages indicate a general acceptance of porn, though there is some frustration about stereotypes in porn.

"While porn has given me space to discover and identify my own sexuality by putting words to feelings, and terms to activities, the ways in which it was presented to me were problematic. Porn is presented to a gay male audience in a very heteronormative way (or maybe to a men-seeking-men audience . . .). It is considered hotter if a gay guy hooks up with a straight guy rather than another gay guy. The idolization of the masculine straight man in gay porn makes the gay man inherently less masculine/more effeminate. For me, this creates tension between masculinity and sexuality. Most gay porn involves two young, white, masculine guys with large penises. If it's any sort of interracial or multiracial porn, it's labeled as black 'thugs' or Hispanic 'papis,' etc. I see this intolerance as coming from *within* the gay community."

—Male, age twenty

Could I Be Addicted to Porn?

Unlike drug users, who need *more* of a drug over time, porn viewers need *different* material to keep them engaged and aroused. The porn industry offers a boundless supply of material to keep up with this demand for variety. Simone Kühn, a lead researcher of a

German study, concludes, "Subjects with a high porn consumption need increasing stimulation to receive the same amount of reward."[3]

I speak on a regular basis with young men who have questions and concerns about their viewing habits or about what they have seen in porn videos. As guys, most of you have not had access to a forum in which to ask these questions before: most sex ed programs avoid the subject, and most parents seem unwilling to broach it. My experience is substantiated by reports from ChildLine, a private and confidential support line in the U.K. that young people can call about any problem they have. The number of calls from boys concerned about the impact of looking at porn has increased dramatically in recent years. ChildLine reports that each year eighteen thousand children and young people visit their discussion boards on exposure to porn.[4]

It is fairly common to hear from college men that they are sometimes unable to get off with a partner whom they find attractive and are confused about how easily they get off watching porn. When I first suggested to a group of college guys that they *consider* what might change if they didn't look at porn for three weeks, I didn't expect any of them to actually try it. But the suggestion that their imagination highlight reel might shift when they didn't have images created for them resonated with two of the guys. Six months later, one of them told me he was still not looking at porn, and the other had abstained for two months and had been choosing to use his imagination more regularly since then. Both reported having greater focus, more energy, more connected sexual encounters, and better erections; they also said they were relying less on porn-driven images while masturbating *and* while having sex.

Whether the images are viewed directly or have simply influenced widespread beliefs about sex, porn has created unrealistic expectations about what female pleasure looks like and how easily it can be achieved. It takes time with a communicative partner to sort out realistic sexual expectations and to get to know one another's bodies. Because hookups are so prevalent in the college social scene, often involving partners who are not particularly familiar with one another, sexual experiences often don't live up to expectations. Many teenage girls and young women report that their male partners ask them why they aren't "like most girls," who remove their pubic hair, scream with pleasure, enjoy anal sex, have small labia, and ejaculate across the room. Young men typically formulate these standards of women's bodies and behaviors after seeing a vast number of women in porn rather than partners of their own.

When the appearance and responses of various partners are not consistent with what they expect, guys may begin to question their own bodies, penis size, and sexual skills. Taking a break from or altogether stopping their consumption of porn has helped some guys work out these issues and concerns. Unfortunately, a number of young men report that the images that got them off when they were first looking at porn seem to linger in their minds. Once certain scenes have elicited a strong response, the activity shown can become a mainstay on the highlight reel. According to a new study published in the *Archives of Sexual Behavior*, "The more pornography a man watches, the more likely he was to use it during sex, request particular pornographic sex acts of his partner, deliberately conjure images of pornography during sex to maintain arousal, and have concerns over his own sexual performance and body image. Further, higher pornography use was negatively associated with enjoying sexually intimate behaviors with a partner."[5]

Violence in Porn

The absence of tenderness, respectful interactions, and consent is a theme in heterosexual porn. According to Enough Is Enough's

"Internet Safety 101" page, "Of the 304 (porn) scenes analyzed, 88.2% contained physical aggression, principally spanking, gagging, and slapping, while 48.7% of scenes contained verbal aggression, primarily name-calling. Perpetrators of aggression were usually male, whereas targets of aggression were overwhelmingly female."[6] Not many years ago, ejaculating on a woman's face (aka the "money shot") was considered an extreme form of degradation. As Gail Dines, author of *Pornland: How Porn Has Hijacked Our Sexuality,* describes, "The ejaculate also marks the woman as used goods, as owned by the man or men who just penetrated her."[7] In her book, Dines quotes porn actor and producer Bill Margold, who explains the money shot in this way: "I'd like to really show what I believe the men want to see: violence against women. I firmly believe that we serve a purpose by showing that. The most violent we can get is the cum shot in the face. Men get off behind that, because they get even with the women they can't have. We try to inundate the world with orgasms in the face."[8]

When viewpoints like this are shared with groups of college guys, most of them recoil in anger and irritation—and for good reason! Very few young men I have interviewed intentionally or consciously started out using porn because they felt anger or resentment toward women. Comments like these made by creators of porn seem to reflect their own lingering bitterness toward women, and they use their medium to reinforce their own views. It is worth disengaging from porn, even if just to decrease the profits of a billion-dollar industry that is manipulating you.

Guys have a strong tendency to seek visual images of sex, and the porn industry capitalizes on that. According to San Francisco psychotherapist Gregory Rowe, "For 90% of men, images are a big source of stimulation."[9] The combination of the male propensity to seek visual images and the increasingly violent acts shown in a large percentage of porn is impacting boys and young men.

In the few years since Margold's quote was published, mainstream porn has become increasingly rife with depictions of brutality against women.

According to a Swedish study of adolescent boys, "The frequency of pornography consumption has been shown to predict various negative outcome measures in humans." The study has shown that boys with daily consumption showed more interest in deviant and illegal types of pornography and more frequently reported the wish to actualize what they saw. In partnerships, a decrease in sexual satisfaction and a tendency to adopt pornographic scripts have been associated with frequent Internet pornography consumption."[10] I hear numerous stories from young women who have found it difficult to convince their male partners that they don't want to be hit, choked, handled roughly, or have their hair pulled. Miscommunication, misinformation, and false assumptions contribute to unhealthy sexual relationships. According to Nancy Jo Sales, author of *American Girls*, "Violent porn that is degrading to women doesn't occur in a vacuum. Its popularity is indicative of a culture in which, despite the welcome gains of women in education and the workforce, women and girls continue to experience sexism and misogyny. The fact that there are still people who would deny this seems indicative of a lack of education."[11]

How Does Porn Consumption Affect Sexual Relationships?

Assumptions go both ways. Some heterosexual guys express surprise and confusion about sexual acts that some female partners ask for, offer, and claim to enjoy. Most of these guys admit that they are just grateful for the opportunity to be naked with a willing partner, and they are therefore nowhere near as selective as they are often expected to be. One guy in a group said if he were asked to dress up as the Easter Bunny to get laid, he would do it. The rest of the guys laughed and nodded in agreement.

Many of the stories I hear from young people, however, indicate that some young women feel the need to compete with porn rather than follow their own desires. Some women offer to perform sexual acts just because they think it is expected and believe they won't be considered attractive unless they do. Such skewed sexual expectations create pressure to engage in sexual behavior to stay sexually relevant among peers, rather than out of genuine desire. Honest communication among partners about their expectations is not common, and the perception of what is "hot" drives a whole lot of sexual behavior that isn't necessarily satisfying for either partner.

> "When porn becomes the only exposure you have to sex and sexuality from the time you are a prepubescent boy to when you have your first partner, it's going to really shape what you think about sex. There are a lot of unfair expectations associated with porn and some that are just simply unrealistic. My partner expected me to expect *her* to be a porn star, so at times I think she tried to act like it to fill the part. It was this cycle of acting on expectations."
>
> —Male, age nineteen

The way the men in hetero porn ravage their partners both vaginally and anally is misleading. A number of gay men have approached me after my college presentations, concerned about their heterosexual peers who are engaging in casual anal sex in a hookup scenario because the men assume, based on porn, that all women enjoy anal sex. They are equally worried that their heterosexual female friends assume they will be expected to have anal sex if they want to be thought of as "hot." Their fears, frankly, are justified: the most frequently asked question I have received from high school girls and college women is, "Why do guys always want to have anal sex?"

Women regularly admit that the pressure to have anal sex is real if you want to stay relevant and be considered hot. This expectation has gone up in recent years, since porn has glorified anal sex. Many women report discomfort, pain, bleeding, and tearing (in some cases needing surgery), as well as yeast infections and STIs in the anus. There is no question that some women enjoy anal sex, but many more engage because they don't want to disappoint. National sex surveys report that in 1992 16 percent of women age eighteen to twenty-four had tried anal sex. That number jumped to 40 percent in 2010.[12] College students are curious because they hear a lot about it, think it is expected, or think it may provide the pleasure that has been elusive for them so far.

The general message from gay men is that heterosexual porn misleads by making anal sex out to be a common heterosexual activity that is "easy and comfortable" and go on to say that a good number of gay men don't enjoy anal sex because they find it painful or had difficult first experiences. There was unanimous agreement in one particular group of gay men when one of the men explained, "Anal sex is a 'process' that can be enjoyable with a well-known partner, however it requires preparation, pacing, communication, and a good supply of water-based lube, which won't break down a condom." While anal sex is pleasurable for some, there are plenty who report anal pain, bleeding, and tearing.

It is not only porn that contributes to misconceptions about anal sex. *Fifty Shades of Grey* and the other books in the trilogy, for example, have temporarily jump-started a lot of adventurous sex for people of all ages. Some students look to the Fifty Shades books for inspiring ideas. Unfortunately, the series has left many heterosexual women feeling inadequate, either for not embracing sexual adventure or for being too willing to take part in sexual acts that are not pleasurable for them. After reading these books, heterosexual boys and men are left confused about what turns women on. On a number of occasions, boys who have read *Fifty Shades of Grey* have asked me if it is true that all women fantasize about being raped and roughly restrained during sex. The influence of this book series, along with Internet porn and mass media depictions of sexuality, contributes to young people's misunderstanding about consensual sex.

I have discussed the Fifty Shades series with a number of people in the "kink" community and the BDSM community (a combination of bondage and discipline and sadism and masochism), as well as with people who express variations on these interests. I had wrongly assumed that members of these groups would consider the books a step toward more mainstream acceptance of their communities and sexual practices. This assumption proved to be wrong, however, because most members of the kink community, BDSM community, and their subgroups view consent as a key element in their sexual choices. As observed by a number of critics, reporters, and mental health professionals who reviewed the franchise harshly, lack of consent is a glaring feature of the relationship between the characters in the Fifty Shades series.

It isn't really clear how the passion for the books and movie is positively influencing the sex lives of the people who sing its praises. Most of the people I have spoken with about the series say that, while it briefly caught their interest and perhaps even spiked their libido, the fantasies described in the books did not actually do much for them in the bedroom. A few innkeepers I know have even noticed a trend of guests leaving behind riding crops and handcuffs at the end of a weekend, indicating that the Fifty Shades fantasy isn't all it is cracked up to be.

So, How Does This All Affect My Sex Life?

According to Alexandra Katehakis, founder and clinical director of the Center for Healthy Sex, "While masturbating to porn, the adolescent brain is being shaped around a sexual experience that is isolating, visceral, and completely void of any love or compassion."[13] While this certainly does not mean that boys who have been viewing porn from a young age have any less desire for love and commitment than those of previous generations, it does indicate that porn contributes to a disconnect between the act of sex and the development of emotional intimacy. Such a disconnect manifests in sexual practices guided by false expectations rather than the desires of the participants.

Many heterosexual guys don't make the connection between the pervasive influence of porn culture and the feelings of some women that they have to compete with porn by "performing" like a porn star. Even though vast numbers of guys are not turned on by hitting or ejaculating on their female partner, they may oblige, taking such requests at face value. Some guys admit that such requests from girls give them bragging rights among their male friends, even though it doesn't feel quite right or satisfy them personally. The lingering worry for some of these young men is that something must be wrong with them if they are not into that kind of sexual activity, and they need to step up their game.

While some guys dream about a partner who acts like an insatiable porn star, others wonder whether women think guys expect that. Women who perceive male partners as expecting or hoping for porn-like experiences and who try to perform to those expectations are more likely to make male pleasure, rather than mutual pleasure, a priority. While communication could clear up these misunderstandings, it continues to be the most avoided sexual practice. Communication, after all, indicates connection, and porn has convinced us that connection is not a requisite for sex. It is primarily in this way that porn has contributed to the hookup culture.

Those on the more sexually adventurous side may consider this perspective limiting and repressive of people's sexual inclinations, but figuring out how to meet one's own basic sexual needs and those of one's partner before engaging in threesomes, role playing, or rough sex empowers a person to find genuine satisfaction in his or her sexual experiences. Many young people assume they will feel satisfied by pushing their sexual boundaries in certain ways, yet end up feeling uncomfortable and unsatisfied. Many, particularly women, tend to just go along with what they think they are supposed to like, or believe that they will learn to like a particular act. They assume that they will catch on with practice, or when they become more comfortable speaking up to their partners. But going along without speaking up about your needs, despite not being satisfied, can quickly become a habit. Not knowing what you like or not being able to tell your partner what you like is a clear sign that you should slow down and figure it out.

Healthy sex is about pleasure given and received by both partners. If sex is consensual and full of communication, and if both parties are finding pleasure, partners should be as sexually adventurous as both agree to be. Unfortunately, I rarely hear about amazing, communicative sex from college students, who often experiment with partners they barely know in a hookup situation. People's fantasies run across a wide spectrum, and you have every right to follow your desires.

Some psychologists argue that critics of porn and *Fifty Shades of Grey* are forgetting that these are about fantasy, and don't depict scenes that most people want to play out. But when girls and college women try to figure out orgasms, the messages from the culture that rough sex may be the way to find true pleasure can be confusing and misleading. College men often admit that they are not comfortable when they are asked to hit, choke, or tie women up, but they oblige because they have heard that women like it and fear they will be rejected if they don't go along. People have every right to push boundaries and experiment, but the rise of BDSM themes in the cultural zeitgeist, paired with a lack of communication between partners, has led to a lot of young people engaging in acts they think will be pleasurable for their partners, but which end up not fulfilling either partner. Bottom line: sex should be mutually satisfying, and communication is the requirement for making that happen.

The prevailing assumption that everyone else seems to have sex figured out factors into the impulsive sexual choices many college students make. Porn has become the first line of sexuality education for young people scrambling for information because it is easily accessible, compelling, and provides anonymity for the viewer. Our timid approach to sexuality education for young kids has resulted in a high number of misguided porn consumers influencing their friends as well as their sexual partners. Our culture is only just beginning to explicitly teach and encourage young people to practice healthy sexual communication, including asking for and giving consent. Those who are willing to admit their limited understanding about sex stand a much better chance of acquiring accurate, clear information. In the next chapter, I will provide tips that will make you more confident with a partner as well as more willing to ask for guidance.

5

Better Sex

How to Find Pleasure and Connection

The tolerance for disconnected sex with unfamiliar partners is what the hookup scene is all about. Many people consider communicating via social media and texts to be an acceptable way to get to know another person, and it is not uncommon for two people to hook up even though they've had very little face-to-face communication. Any kind of sexual encounter makes you vulnerable, both physically and emotionally. Sex can be awkward in the best of circumstances, and there is no app that can rescue us from the unease of being emotionally and physically naked with another person. No matter how hard people work to justify hooking up with someone they don't know well, it is a recipe for a disconnected sexual experience.

A healthy sexual encounter involves a strong connection between partners. Dr. Marty Klein, certified sex therapist and author of *Sexual Intelligence*, says, "I see an increasing number of people who don't feel comfortable doing one thing at a time anymore. And that's bad for sex. Because—assuming you're with someone you want to be with, and they're pleased to be with you—there's only (a few) things you actually need to enjoy sex: Focus. Attention. Engagement."[1]

It has become a common idea that young people can't be encouraged to focus on anything or anyone for too long because they are busy with so many commitments. When I speak to groups of high school or college students about casual sex and the hookup scene, some of them ask questions about how to balance their desire to have sex with the fact that they don't want a committed relationship because they have such busy lives. I have heard girls claim they couldn't possibly have sex in any sort of committed way because it will get the way of their desire for a career. This attitude that a meaningful relationship is incompatible with attaining other life goals contributes to the acceptance of hookups, and casual sex seems to have joined the list of extracurricular activities like athletics and campus clubs.

> "The more students talk about hooking up, the clearer it becomes that it has less to do with excitement or even attraction than with checking a box off a long list of tasks, like homework or laundry. And while hookup sex is supposed to come with no strings attached, it nonetheless creates an enormous amount of stress and drama among participants."
> —Donna Freitas, *The End of Sex: How Hookup Culture Is Leaving a Generation Unhappy, Sexually Unfulfilled, and Confused About Intimacy*

If descriptions of most college sex made it sound amazing and fulfilling, I would not have bothered to write this book. While people may be thrilled with the opportunity to hook up with a certain person or to hook up at all, the actual sexual encounters don't get rave reviews. College students have a high tolerance for sex ranging from cringe-worthy to slightly sloppy to halfway decent to fine. Optimism about the next great hookup, or the social credibility that goes along with a hookup, keeps people in the game. One prevailing belief is that sex will get better with more practice and that the "hookup club" is something in which students are expected to participate even if it doesn't get beyond sloppy.

Sex should not only be consensual but should also be pleasurable and fun for both participants. Female pleasure has not been much of a priority and seems to be left for people to figure out on their own, despite the fact that women have more complicated anatomy. As a woman, if you are going to be having sex, you should have the opportunity to experience orgasms. It takes work to learn how your pleasure zones work, a process that is made difficult when you have a series of different partners, or partners who do not know you well. Having sex with fewer partners and making more careful choices in your partners can improve the quality of your sexual relationships, but the expectation for sex with random partners is so prevalent that bucking the trend requires a great deal of social courage.

As a speaker who talks openly about healthy sexuality, I find that students are overwhelmingly grateful when I present honest, specific, and helpful information about sex and pleasure. There's an unspoken pressure for all of you to figure sex out on your own—most of you seem to feel that you are expected to either know the answers or be smart enough to acquire the necessary skills and information on your own. Porn has become the main sexuality resource for many young men, and this has an indirect influence on heterosexual women.

When you have accurate information from reliable sources and you know your partner well enough to communicate openly, sex improves dramatically. The idea that sexual mileage will lead you to deeper sexual understanding is misguided (so you should probably stop listening to that friend of yours who claims to know all the tricks). If you repeatedly have sloppy sex or sex you just consider "fine," then the bar will likely stay pretty low. What we practice becomes our practice. A fulfilling sexual relationship can happen between partners who are willing to be vulnerable and communicate with one another. If you think it would be awkward to actually *talk* with your partner, take a step back—that's a clear indicator that getting naked with that person isn't a good idea. Affirmative consent requires verbal communication, as does a mutually pleasurable sexual experience. Sex can be especially fulfilling and pleasurable when you care for one another and share a respectful connection that enables you to communicate openly.

Female Pleasure Doesn't Just Happen

As Al Vernacchio, author of *For Goodness Sex,* suggests, "If you can't look a person in the eye and talk about it, you shouldn't be doing it."[2] Some college students report that they find it "annoying" to be expected to talk with their partners. As one student put it, "Talking is a huge positive, but it can easily become a negative since it's so often awkward when people say what they want or ask you what you want. It seems like if we're good we should just know without saying." This idea that people who are good at sex should know what they are doing is the main reason so many young people are off track—and they stay off track waiting for their sex skills to improve or for psychic powers to lead them to a dynamic, earth-shattering sex life with someone they can't even talk to. Without communication, great sex will be a long wait.

> "I hadn't expected that my first sexual experience would be awkward, wouldn't last long, and that neither of us would know what we were doing."
>
> —Male, age nineteen

A huge obstacle for finding sexual satisfaction for women is the fact that figuring out female pleasure is challenging, whether you are alone or with a partner. Each woman's pleasure zones are unique and don't respond consistently to the same approach to stimulation, so communication and ongoing adaptation are a must for her partner, whether that partner is male or female. This is why porn and the friend who gets laid all the time are unreliable resources. Porn portrays female pleasure unrealistically—as if being pounded is what women need in order to reach orgasm or squirting across the room is a sign that a top-notch orgasm has been achieved. The number of college women who admit they fake orgasms indicates that their partners aren't really getting an honest read on how the encounter went. Anyone interested in giving true pleasure to women should find a trusted female friend or group of platonic female friends and ask them openly what they experience with their sexual partners. Women should do the same with trusted guy friends.

> "When I have sex with boys, I am not very nervous at all. I don't have an overwhelming amount of experience, but I also feel like I know what I'm doing and can be confident and not self-conscious. With girls, I have very little experience so I'm a bit less comfortable starting sexual relationships."
>
> —Female, age twenty

The assumption that women can easily satisfy female partners may lead to hurt feelings and confusion for both partners. Female pleasure is a moving target because each woman's pleasure zones are different and seem to be constantly changing based on hormonal cycles and a number of other factors. According to men and women who have sex with women, there isn't a dependable approach to bringing a woman to orgasm. Women need to understand how their own pleasure zones work, so they can guide their partner. Guiding requires communication. Acknowledging that female pleasure is elusive and unreliable is a great way to open up good communication with your partner.

Common traits among sexually knowledgeable and satisfied people include comfort with not knowing, willingness to ask questions, the courage to talk with your partner, and openness to information from reliable resources. While helpful and accurate information is available from a variety of resources, any online search (the most common approach) requires that you sort through a lot of misleading, highly viewed pornographic material to find much-needed reliable information and guidance.

Cindy's Take

One guy summarized something I have been hearing for decades: "I had been searching for the clitoris for years. Asking would have made me feel like an idiot. Assuming I should know, I pumped or rubbed a little harder in the mysterious zone I had heard about. Finally, I had a girlfriend who told me, 'You just can't know.' This took the pressure off, gave me permission to ask for help, and my sex life has been amazing since."

Sex Under the Influence

Some people think that they are not responsible for what they say or do while under the influence of alcohol or drugs. Hooking up with a random person requires some level of disconnection from one's healthy sexual self as well as disconnection from your partner. Drinking is an accepted and common way to facilitate social interactions. One college sophomore sums up the accepted link between alcohol and sex in college: "In my first year of college, alcohol was always involved in finding sexual partners, but the more causal factor, I believe, is the party atmosphere, which offers a casual place for classmates and people of similar ages and interests to come together and mingle. The presence of alcohol merely provided me with an excuse to be outgoing."

Many hookups start through social media or dating apps, with follow-up interactions via text. This can create a false sense of "knowing" a person. If you have only ever communicated with a partner through texts, awkwardness is almost guaranteed when you ultimately find yourselves naked together. No matter how you frame a sexual encounter, it is, and should be, an emotionally and physically vulnerable experience. Being under the influence of alcohol (or, less commonly, a drug) is the most common way people attempt to make the encounter more comfortable. True courage requires that we open ourselves up to a connection with another person, to the risk of rejection, and to emotional vulnerability—and it requires that you ask for consent or guidance from your partner.

> "I am just tired of having a relationship based off sex. I want to be intimate with a person without sex. Hooking up makes me feel undervalued and not appreciated because the person only wants me for sex."
>
> —Female, age nineteen

Unfortunately, the ability to communicate won't magically land on you in adulthood or when you get into a long-term commitment. I have interviewed thousands of adults in long-term relationships who are still not speaking up and asking for what they would enjoy sexually, willing to endure their fate of below-average sex. Good sex takes work and courage. The sooner you face that and get to work, the better your sex life will be.

Sending Nudes—A Big Deal?

The trend of sending nude photos and dick pics through Snapchat and other platforms reflects a lack of self-consciousness that has emerged over the last decade or so. Sexual acts and images are so commonplace that people want to be part of it. Internet porn has contributed to the ways people sexualize one another and themselves through social media. Many women claim that it is empowering to hook up with whomever they want, or send nude photos or share vidoes of themselves masturbating. I hear young women say, "I am proud of my body and should be able to hook up or send nudes without being slut shamed." Our culture puts a lot of pressure on young women to keep up with expectations, to appear sexually bold, to seek social credibility, and to be "hot." Sending nude pics is the quickest way to gain the approval and attention of the gate-keepers of certain social circles who decide who is hot, worthy, and relevant. Some women respond to requests for nudes because they hope to be the focus of a guy's masturbation rather than porn. In reality, most guys will be looking at porn anyway.

When a guy claims that he will keep a photo or video private or he promises to delete it, most women believe him. Some guys do keep them private. But numerous college-age men admit they have access to extensive collections of nude photos online, keep a stash on their phones, and don't hesitate to share them with friends. In some cases, a guy will distribute the photos as a dare, to get revenge on a woman who rejected him, or to shame a woman who treated a friend of his badly. Who has the "power" once the nudes are distributed to other people? Aside from photos and videos, it is fairly common for guys to share Excel spreadsheets and Google docs with lists of women's names and the sexual acts in which they are willing to partake, together with ratings.

If the righteous claims of sexual empowerment and liberation were matched with full knowledge of one's capacity for orgasms and the confidence to verbally guide a partner to provide pleasure, I would be more convinced. More commonly, I hear college women talk about their misunderstanding about female pleasure, their discomfort asking about it, and how awkward it would be to discuss with a partner. I blame the culture for this disconnect. As a society, we are still fearful of teaching girls and women about their capacity for pleasure, but at the same time we tolerate the endless sexualization of women in the media. These mixed messages from our culture have contributed to young women developing a false sense of empowerment and confusion about their worth based on their willingness to share nudes and engage in the hookup culture.

In the conclusion of *American Girls*, Nancy Jo Sales reminds us that "for girls now to model themselves in the image of pornography... is for them to embrace their own disempowerment."[3]

Why Is There Such a Rush to Hook Up?

"Hooking up" may mean simply kissing or it may refer to some combination or variation of oral sex, intercourse, or anal sex. "Hooking up" is a conveniently vague term that allows people to be a part of the scene at some level and maintain privacy at the same time. It can ensure avoidance of scrutiny and pressure if you and your chosen partner didn't really do much more than cuddle or make out. If two people had intercourse, saying they hooked up can keep judgment at bay by avoiding details. There is often an imbalance of expectations and motivations for each of the people hooking up. Sometimes the imbalance inspires one of them to share details with other people as a form of social currency, a way to gain status among friends, or to publicly shame their partner.

During a group discussion, a high school sophomore girl said, "If you hook up once, that means one of the people is interested. If you hook up twice, that means both are interested. If you hook up a third time, then it's 'a thing.'" All the girls in the group nodded in agreement, as most high school *and* college students do when

I repeat this statement. Backward dating seems to be the way it goes, despite the fact that recent research shows that many young people—both male and female—are equally interested in relationships and often hope that hooking up may lead to a relationship.

The perception that everyone is hooking up creates a lot of pressure for you to be a part of the club. One senior in college sums up a common feeling: "Self-doubt can make a hookup a negative experience. Generally, I worry about not having enough hookups since it seems like everyone else does it all the time, and I worry about not being 'good in bed' when I do." The perception that everyone is doing it drives people to seek a hookup with more intensity, which drives standards down. Another senior added, "Some peoples' self-worth is dependent on them hooking up with someone. They go out to a party looking for it and then it can turn to desperation."

> "My boyfriend and I were hookup buddies. Over time we took the sexual aspects of our relationship out and started to get to know each other. The negative part is that I constantly felt insecure because he originally only wanted me for sex. It was a hard adjustment to get used to the idea that he wanted me for me."
>
> —Female, age twenty-one

Many first-year female students hook up with older guys because they feel honored to be chosen and want to be part of the scene. Kids who grew up with restrictive parents may find that the freedom of college inspires them to lose their virginity to "get it over with." Some of you seek stress relief or sexual release. Many of you stumble into a hookup because you are too drunk to be aware of what you really want, while others among you blame the hookup on alcohol in order to avoid judgment from peers. Because female orgasms are uncommon in a hookup scenario, it is apparent that the hookup isn't really about sexual satisfaction for many women. And I have learned from young men—and this has been confirmed by Donna Freitas's research—that even though most guys get off during a hookup, many report feeling emotionally unfulfilled by the experience.[4]

Many people report that hookups rarely end up being what they expected and hoped for. The drama that goes along with it can be exhausting. Maintaining a balance of appearing interested enough but not caring too much takes energy. Coming across as caring too much can repel an interested partner. It is risky to open up about your feelings or express anything particularly intimate because you might appear to be "obsessed" or needy.

Shouldn't an Experienced Partner Be Able to Give Me an Orgasm?

What you practice becomes your practice. If you think you will "gain experience" by hooking up a lot, you will ultimately discover that mileage does not usually deepen sexual understanding, knowledge, or confidence. Hooking up with a lot of partners can actually reinforce ineffective techniques, unless partners are willing to ask for and give feedback. The assumption that "experienced" partners know what they are doing deters some people from giving feedback. Listening to experienced men describe what they think women love is disconcerting. They often describe the very techniques and moves that women in groups complain about. I have interviewed a number of outspoken women who are mystified why their partners treat them roughly even though they are clear they are not interested in rough sex. Hundreds of women I work with complain openly about the painful jackhammer pounding they are subjected to with so many men.

It is fairly common for women to recognize that their male partner is fumbling around trying to find their clitoris, but they don't speak up and don't quite get there as a result. College women I interview individually and in groups typically say they are reluctant to give a male partner feedback even if the sex is awful, particularly if he is very experienced. The most common reason they give is that they don't want to hurt the guy's feelings. For years, I was aghast at women's willingness to forgo their own satisfaction in order to please their male partners, and tried to rally them to own their pleasure by figuring out for themselves what they liked and then guiding their partners. When the involvement is a one-time or short-term thing, though, most don't think it is worth it.

The claim that heterosexual guys don't care about female pleasure is not true. There's the occasional jerk who doesn't care, but that is not the prevailing attitude I have heard from most heterosexual guys over the years. Most guys admit to borderline desperation for input, guidance, and direction from their partners, but they feel they are supposed to know what they are doing already and therefore they rummage around, trying to figure it out. Teammates, fraternity brothers, and friends depend on their sexually experienced peers to give them information. Unfortunately, unless your experienced friend has had a very comfortable and communicative partner, he is at risk of repeating what he has learned from porn and the "experienced" guys who gave *him* misinformation. Because of the stigma around asking for guidance from a partner and the fact that both men and women are reluctant to speak up, people are having a lot of below-average sex, which internalizes a low standard for what sex is supposed to be like.

When women know their pleasure zones, they make their own pleasure more of a priority and are more willing to speak up and guide their partners (see "Some Facts About Female Pleasure" at the end of this chapter). This is one reason female masturbation should be encouraged, but unfortunately there is still a stigma around it. According to one sexuality educator and school counselor, "If girls and women find masturbation more 'creepy' than sex with someone they barely know, that should inspire them to reconsider their choices." Female pleasure zones are elusive because the physical terrain around the clitoris is complicated, and pleasure education is not valued in our culture. Almost all college women and heterosexual men are quite curious about female pleasure yet they avoid discussing it with their hookup partners. Authentic sexual liberation is about knowing your sexual needs.

I Thought Hooking Up Would Be Empowering

The decision to opt out of the hookup scene is becoming more widely accepted. Those who stay in the hookup game maintain enough optimism to accept that a few unhealthy choices and mistakes are part of the process of growing up and figuring out what they want in a relationship. Setbacks can help recalibrate standards and inspire more appropriate choices. Experts agree, however, that repeated choices and behaviors can create patterns—all the relationships you have impact your subsequent relationships. If you put up with abusive friends, you may choose a partner who treats you in a similar way. Repeated casual sex without personal connection or honest communication can influence relationship expectations.

> "No matter what people say, it's hard to have a no-strings-attached hookup. I hope for more ownership of my body and confidence in my body. I am looking for more meaningful connections with potential for sustained happiness rather than random hookups that leave me feeling alone and empty."
>
> —Female, age twenty-seven

Hooking up with a stranger, acquaintance, or friend diminishes the chance of an emotionally or physically fulfilling experience. The "good in bed" myth perpetuates the idea that good sex is reserved for people who just know a lot, have had a lot of experience, or are desirable people who look like celebrities and act like porn stars. In reality, every person of any age or at any level of sexual experience has the capacity to be an amazing sexual partner for a person with whom they share a strong connection, trust, and respect. These factors, however, are not part of the hookup equation, which is based more on physical connection rather than on intimacy. Al Vernacchio has wise advice for young people: "The best sexual activity doesn't come from a manual or a list of instructions. It comes from knowing your body, knowing your partner's body, and communicating about what brings both people pleasure. That's what we all should do when we engage in sexual activity."[5]

Knowing your partner's body requires communication. Some women say they are too busy for any sort of commitment but still want to have sex. An unfortunate result of this attitude is that *very* few of these women are experiencing orgasms in their hookups. Some assume hooking up will help them figure it out. Some decide to buck the double standard—guys who hook up a lot are praised for being players while girls are called sluts—and approach hooking up as an empowering act that proves they can engage in sex the same way guys do. When asked how this approach feels over time, these women often say it is unfulfilling and not what they had hoped for. During a presentation for college men and women, one woman stood up to tell the whole group that women should do what they want and hook up with as many guys as they want. She was forceful and fiery in her statements. As she concluded her rage about the injustice, she started crying, admitted that it wasn't satisfying, and said she was just mad at guys who can hook up without getting attached and are not judged.

While there are guys who treat hooking up as a higher form of masturbation, that is not the case for most. The generalization that guys don't care about relationships and just want sex is actually not true. Recent research aligns with what I have heard from young men for years: during her research on college hookup culture, author Donna Freitas discovered, "There are many men out there at colleges and universities across America who are sad, ashamed, and/or ambivalent about hooking up and the sex they are having; who wish for long-term relationships, dating, love, and romance; and who feel that their sex lives are actually pretty unfulfilling, even bad and embarrassing. If they want to be regarded as 'real men' or 'guys,' however, they also feel they must go along with the hookup culture without complaints."[6]

The claims that hooking up is empowering and sexually liberating don't hold up for most individuals over time. Many people in their twenties and thirties, particularly women, have a different lens when they reflect on what they perceived as "empowering" sexual experiences in high school and early college. Many recent college graduates cringe as they describe being disrespected, objectified, or even used by guys when they were younger, and regret their claims that the choice was empowering. A prevailing sentiment among these women is that they regret getting caught up in the random hookup scene, and they insist that I encourage younger women and men to make the choice to avoid it. The pattern of women and men questioning what they were getting out of sex and wishing they had made different choices is reflected in national surveys and in the findings of many sexuality educators.

LGBTQ People Often Feel Excluded

The hookup scene on many campuses has a heteronormative vibe, which can feel exclusive to LGBTQ people. The LGBTQ communities on many campuses are small, which can make it challenging to get sexually involved at any level. Dating apps help some LGBTQ people meet others in a wider geographic area, but that carries some complications—and sometimes the app matches people on campus who don't want to be matched.

One student articulates clearly the personal and broader issues of the hookup culture:

> It is harder to find other queer people on a lot of college campuses because the pool of people to draw from and interact with is smaller. This is magnified on our campus because we are isolated. As a nonbinary person, I don't feel like I fit in, even among the binary LGBTQ students. The hookup scene is particularly hard for genderqueer individuals. I have a very complicated relationship with my body, especially my genitals. I am still figuring out how to be comfortable with my body. Therefore, my partner(s) really need(s) to know that about me and be patient with me to help me through the dysphoria and avoid intensifying it. Therefore, hooking up is not that realistic for me, because patience and understanding do not define hookup culture.

It is also challenging for openly gay men or lesbians to respect sexual partners of the same gender who want to hook up but claim to be heterosexual. Four years of negotiating the difference between questioning, experimenting, and strongly considering led to frustration for this young woman:

> As a queer woman, it gets super annoying and hurtful to hook up with women who aren't comfortable with their sexuality. I've had fun hookups with women who want to experiment. I don't mind until it becomes a consistent thing and I start to feel like I have to hide emotions because I don't want to make her think it's serious. There is a gap between extremely

outwardly gay girls (kind of butch looking or masculine) and then closeted girls. I'm not usually attracted to the former and the latter are both hard to find or complicated to deal with considering they are just experimenting.

What Creates Positive Hookup Experiences?

For a long time, many college students claimed the hookup culture was empowering and liberating. Anyone who questioned it was considered an antisex buzzkill who sided with the administration and parents. The conversation has broadened in recent years, however. Now that more people are feeling comfortable questioning the hookup culture and admitting that it isn't particularly empowering or fulfilling a lot of the time, we are hearing the nuanced perspectives of those who have genuinely enjoyed hooking up or found a version that works for them for now.

Most college students admit that the sloppy, drunk hookup with a random person is unfulfilling. Others argue that hooking up with a good friend or a person you know well without commitment can be fun and interesting. Some hookup experiences that have been described to me as great and fulfilling have involved a quirky adventure such as a middle-of-the-night hike, running through sprinklers, or climbing trees rather than being just about the sex. World travelers describe connecting on a deep level through conversations that last hours or even a full day as a more sped-up version of dating that ultimately led to a mutually respectful and enjoyable hookup.

In their *New York* magazine article "Heirs to the Sexual Revolution," Lauren Kern and Noreen Malone gathered many perspectives about college sex from a spectrum of students. Some decide to opt out after engaging in the hookup scene, and a few find hooking up easier than commitment, choosing to have sex with good friends and maybe find love in the process. The authors concluded, "College students also share a sense of optimism about the many ways for young people to explore their own identities and sexuality, to figure out who they are and whom they want to love."[7] My hope is that the sexual exploration people choose to engage in includes communication, consent, and sexual fulfillment for both participants.

"Adventurous" Sex May Not Help You Learn About Pleasure

Learning about sexual pleasure by yourself before engaging in a sexual encounter with another person is both wise and the safest kind of sex. While boys and men seem to begin masturbating as a matter of course, this is not the case for many women. A fair number of young women are taking part in threesomes or foursomes before they have figured out how their pleasure zones work and how to communicate comfortably with one partner, much less with two or more partners. People will make their own decisions about what they enjoy and engage in sexually, but hopefully they get a chance to discover what they find pleasurable before they choose to swing from a trapeze with a double-headed dildo and jump into sex with multiple partners at one time.

> "Learning about healthy sexual boundaries and connecting with one's body before engaging in sexual relationships is a more sure path to making conscious, empowering sexual choices that align with your authentic self."
> —Sarah Haykel, director and life coach at Salsa for the Soul

There is a lot of pressure to engage in adventurous sex. For women in particular, there is tremendous pressure to have an insatiable sexual appetite and be sexually daring. I hear from women who recount a fairly extensive list of adventurous sexual experiences—including anal sex, role-playing, rough sex, and threesomes—in hookup scenarios rather than with a committed partner or even someone they know well. When I ask these women about orgasms, they consistently express uncertainty about how to make that happen or assume that their orgasms are the responsibility of their partners.

When I speak to groups of women, the Q&A usually reveals that only a handful out of every fifty seem to know how their own pleasure zones work. I am sure there are a few more who are sexually fulfilled but may be less comfortable talking about it. Almost all of the women in these groups are eager for information and guidance, and some want clarification about how to have orgasms. There are always a few knowledgeable women who are willing to educate their peers, while others quietly assume everyone else has "figured out" how to have pleasurable sex. While there can be a wide variety of pleasurable sexual contact that does not involve female orgasms, it is clear that the sex many people are having is not particularly pleasurable or emotionally fulfilling for either partner.

Even though most guys are getting off in a hookup, many report that the encounters are emotionally unfulfilling. The fact that many guys are looking for connection is contrary to the generalizations we hear about guys and sex. I also hear from college men that unless they care about a person, masturbation can sometimes be easier than hooking up because it requires less energy than "dealing" with another person.

"Sometimes I would rather just beat off to porn rather than hook up with a girl. It is kind of a hassle to have sex with a girl who comments about being self-conscious about her body. I would never notice if she didn't keep bringing it up."

—Male, age twenty

SOME FACTS ABOUT FEMALE PLEASURE

Despite the complicated nature of female orgasms, few parents or sex ed programs teach kids how female orgasms work. Generally, women are lucky if they figure out how to have orgasms or have friends or partners who educate them. Add this lack of education to the misleading representations of sexuality in pornography, and you have a recipe for misunderstanding. If more people understood the following points about female pleasure, perhaps they would improve their sexual communication and find more pleasure in sex.

1. The sole purpose of the clitoris is pleasure. What makes the clitoris elusive is the fact that it lives under a hood, which is like a garage protecting the clitoris's eight thousand nerves (double the number found on the penis). The bulb of the clitoris is very sensitive. The shaft of the clitoris is slightly less sensitive and a good place to stimulate if the bulb of the clitoris is too sensitive at first. The clitoral legs extend into the walls of the vagina, adding some sensitivity, though sensation there is not as intense as it is in the area around the clitoris or the vulva, depending on the woman's individual anatomy. The clitoral hood is a handy feature that protects the clitoris from stimulation from clothing.

2. An estimated 70 to 80 percent of women do not experience clitoral orgasms with penetration alone. This has led many women to think they are not capable of orgasms, though most women are, with additional stimulation from another source—either a finger or a vibrator. A woman or her partner can lend a helping hand during penetration.

3. The average time men take to reach orgasm is usually much shorter than that required for women (a few minutes for men versus

an average of ten to twenty minutes for women). This poses a timing issue for heterosexual couples unless there is good communication or use of foreplay to help both partners experience maximum pleasure. There is an assumption that two women can give each other orgasms easily, but every woman's pleasure zones respond differently—what brings pleasure for one woman is not only different from other women, but it could change each day, each cycle, and as she ages. It is helpful for a woman to guide her partner verbally and clearly. I always say, "Be the GPS for your partner."

4. Erogenous zones vary from person to person, and they also shift. Communication is required to know if one's partner enjoys being caressed on her neck, earlobe, hip, feet, nipples, elbow, or wherever. Remember, erogenous zones move camp; "reliable erogenous zone" is a contradiction in terms. Figuring out a partner's desires requires adaptation and communication every time.

5. Located about two inches up the front wall of the vagina, the G-spot works differently for every woman. Stimulation of the G-spot can help arousal progress for some women. Some have a completely unresponsive G-spot, some have a G-spot that is responsive every time she is penetrated, and other women have a G-spot that is responsive some of the time. Some women develop a more responsive G-spot as they age. Stimulation of this area can lead to more intense arousal and cause a tensing of the vaginal walls. Some refer to this tightening as a "vaginal orgasm," not to be confused with the "clitoral orgasm." Vaginal orgasms are a wonderful sensation, but the clitoral orgasm is much more intense, resulting in a dopamine rush.

Knowing how to create fulfillment for both partners is an important part of engaging sexually with a partner. Unfortunately, the sexual learning curve is often glacially slow in the realm of hookup sex because people assume that sexual fulfillment and understanding will align if you just keep at the sex part. Making choices and handling consequences are part of growing up, but few people reach the level of sexual satisfaction and understanding they expect when they choose to engage in the hookup culture.

I urge you to aim for more personal satisfaction in your sexual encounters by considering fewer partners and choosing them more carefully. For those who are determined to engage in the hookup scene and enjoy casual sex, muster the courage to communicate clearly about consent, pleasure, protection, and birth control, and pay attention to how hooking up impacts you emotionally. Heartbreak and disappointment are part of the process of learning about relationships, whether you have casual sex or are in a committed relationship. Your intention may be to avoid drama, but recognize that, no matter how well you communicate expectations to a hookup partner, some level of drama may find its way into the situation. Remember that alcohol is often intended to facilitate communication by easing nerves and loosening inhibitions, but it can create a false sense of connection that complicates sexual relationships.

6

Alcohol

How to Have a Smarter Relationship with Substances in College

The combination of sex and alcohol is nothing new for most of you. The desire for sex and a desire to be part of the hookup scene lead to reliance on alcohol to ease social awkwardness. Drinking alcohol lowers inhibitions, and the hookup scene flourishes under these conditions—very intentionally. There is an unspoken social contract that most people at parties are open to engaging in excessive drinking and casual sex. Social media and word of mouth help normalize the behaviors and feed the widespread perception that "everyone is doing it." Getting drunk and hooking up is considered a rite of passage that young people take lightly (or appear to take lightly).

> "I rely heavily on alcohol and social events involving alcohol to get the confidence to start relationships and facilitate hookups. In high school, I didn't really hook up with people until I started drinking and was never in a serious relationship. Alcohol lowers inhibitions. I feel more confident and less nervous when I drink."
>
> —Female, age nineteen

The messages you internalized about sex, alcohol, and drugs when you were growing up shape your attitudes and influence your decisions when you are on your own. While you were still living at home, your parents no doubt tried to help you develop a strong inner compass that would guide you in working through difficult decisions later. Heading to college, to work, or on a gap year represents a dramatic shift to a much more independent existence away from the rules and consequences enforced by adults at home or at boarding school. Stumbles, failures, problems, and setbacks are to be expected—these experiences provide great learning opportunities and build resilience. Students who land on a college campus unprepared can easily get swept up in the social scene because it is the first time they have experienced freedom.

Experts agree that delaying use of drugs and alcohol through the teenage years is beneficial for developing brains. According to neuroscientist Dr. Frances E. Jensen, it is important for teenagers to know that addiction works more efficiently in the adolescent brain, just as it's easier for teens to learn a new fact.[1] The brain is still developing through college and beyond.

Why Is There So Much Pressure to Drink in College?

When people put pressure on you to drink, you may assume that they will only include you if you partake. The people who are motivated to drink because of social awkwardness or the need to belong are also those most likely to pressure others to drink. Some people want others to join them to justify their own choices—to legitimize the idea that heavy drinking is acceptable, and the way to have fun. Some heavy drinkers rally others to join because they want to avoid judgment and revealing their true selves. When people indulge together in heavy drinking, they create a false sense of connection while maintaining emotional distance.

"I would like to see changes in the social scene. I wish people would ask each other out on dates or date before hooking up. Many couples on campus stemmed from drunken hookups. Why can't it be the other way around? Start dating and then get physical. It is too bad alcohol is always involved."

—Female, age twenty-one

Stress is a contributing factor to heavy drinking for people of all ages. College students have such busy academic and social lives that they tend to live in a state of exhaustion trying to keep up with all their obligations and not miss out on the social scene. Getting drunk is an acceptable way to unplug from responsibilities and pressures from external sources (professors, advisors, parents, coaches) and internal sources (fear, social anxiety, high expectations). There are layers of contributing factors woven into the accepted drinking scene. The first six weeks of college are the time when most students are vulnerable to heavy drinking and the hookup scene. This period—during the first six weeks of the first year of college—is also the time when women are at the highest risk of being sexually assaulted. This is presumably also true for men, though it is harder to get statistics about rates of assault for men because they are generally less likely to report the incidents.

Stress puts people at risk for using alcohol, drugs, or sex to check out, disconnect, or numb their feelings. Alcohol use and binge drinking are common practice for college students, and are not only accepted but also encouraged in many environments. Binge drinkers will find plenty of company in a party scene. But on most campuses there are other options for relieving stress and having fun. According to one student: "There is more to do on campus than getting shitty drunk. Although it may seem like everyone you know is getting drunk and having the time of their lives, that is not the reality." There are other fun things to do, and you may find some friends who would leap at a suggestion to do one of those activities rather than default to the standard party scene.

For some people, the change or loss of the identity they had throughout middle and high school can make the transition to college stressful. If you were a star athlete, a lead in all the plays, one of the brightest kids in your class, or a standout in any activity, going to college can make you feel average because you find yourself surrounded by many talented, bright people. Anyone who is used to being noticed may find this dramatic shift in identity difficult to handle. Entering a large population of students can add to the angst of anonymity. By maintaining awareness of how this transition is affecting you, however, you can work to establish a healthy new identity.

Some of you will struggle with being less visible in your new, expanded community and may end up seeking attention by becoming a big-time partier. Being the reliable drunk who gets the most laughs and generates a lot of stories among friends can be a way to feel popular. The healthier option (for both your liver and your mental state) is finding a community within the larger community. Every college has a variety of clubs, organizations, intramural sports, or interesting classes that can provide you with a sense of community outside the party scene. Finding a workout buddy or hanging out with a group of folks with whom you share interests gives you the opportunity to connect without alcohol. Be aware that older students may struggle to welcome younger students into their groups without using their access to alcohol as the connector. When alcohol is the primary means of connection for a group, however, it can impair the development of authentic, lasting friendships between people in that group.

The Challenges of Drinking in Moderation

It takes some effort to find fun gatherings of nondrinkers in college. There are nondrinking gatherings and activities, but it means you may be without some of your good friends. Attending parties as a nondrinker, or abstaining from drinking on a particular night, may take some willpower, but there is more support among your peers than you realize. One senior in college suggests, "You don't have to do anything you aren't comfortable with because most people are understanding. I have gone out some nights with a bottle of water. When I say no to their offer of a drink, they respect that and even tell me that they respect that I don't want to drink that night."

Choosing not to drink will be easier with the support of your healthy crew—the reliable, close friends who accept you as your true self—which can make it easier to fend off the few aggressive partygoers who can't let it go. Some people can't bear the thought of someone staying sober at a party and won't let up trying to get you to engage, especially if they are already drunk. You may get lots of questions about your choice not to drink. Most people eventually get used to your presence as a nondrinker and will stop bothering you. The fact that I'm a lifelong nondrinker has not deterred some close friends from pouring me a glass of wine or trying to hand me a beer, because it is just what people do to make others feel welcome in social situations.

Drinking moderately can actually be harder than not drinking at all. Sometimes the party environment makes it easy to lose track of your consumption and, before you know it, you are completely intoxicated. The key is to have a plan before you go to a party, stick to your plan, and go home when you start to get annoyed by intoxicated people. Current college students report that there are always a few students attending parties who choose not to drink alcohol, but excessive drinking is the norm.

Marijuana

Many people insist that marijuana is natural and better for you than alcohol. Even where it is legal, it is against the law for people under twenty-one years of age, though that is not slowing down anyone who wants to get high. Current brain research confirms that developing brains are much more vulnerable to addiction. Kids who start using marijuana before fourteen years of age are four times more likely to become addicted,[2] and kids whose parents have a positive attitude toward marijuana are five times more likely to use it by eighth grade.[3]

Look closely at the recent research before you relax about smoking or ingesting pot. According to the University of Mississippi's Potency Monitoring Project, "The average potency of marijuana has jumped from 3.4 percent THC in 1993 to 12.3 percent THC in 2012. Scientists at the lab say they've seen samples as high as 36 percent."[4] Smoking or vaporizing marijuana is a quick way to get high. Smoking marijuana, however, exposes people to toxins and tars that cause respiratory problems.

Consuming marijuana through ingestion (edibles) means that effects may not be felt for forty-five to ninety minutes, because the substance must be digested. The effects last longer, but they take time to manifest. This has proven problematic for inexperienced and impatient users, who ingest too much because they expect to feel the effects sooner.

People who use marijuana tend to show a decrease in motivation, interest, and focus. Pilot studies using simulators show acute impairment for two to six hours after use and carryover effects for up to twenty-four hours.[5] It is estimated that 9 percent of people who use marijuana will become dependent on it, and that number rises to about 17 percent for those who start using when they are young (in their teens), and to 25 to 50 percent among daily users.[6] Although addiction to marijuana is generally considered to be mental rather than physical, it is still serious and debilitating.

Developing Social Confidence Without Alcohol

Four out of five college students drink alcohol, and about half of college students binge drink.[7] I've traveled to a variety of campuses over the past decade, and it is evident that those of you who landed at college uninformed and unaware of the social pressures surrounding alcohol use find it challenging to navigate the social scene. According to the office of the vice provost for university life at the University of Pennsylvania, "The average college student spends $900 a year on alcohol and $450 a year on books!"[8]

Many of you assume that, by the time you are finished with college, you will have it all figured out, sexually and socially. The reality is that sexual and social comfort is a lifelong process. Depending on alcohol to feel more comfortable in conversations with potential sexual partners is likely to become a habit rather than lead to social ease. Repetition and practice ingrain behaviors. The tendency to use alcohol to keep feelings of awkwardness at bay doesn't magically disappear after you've been doing it for years. Practicing sober courage in social and sexual situations is more likely to lead to genuine comfort and confidence.

"I wish I had known more about how to interact with girls. It takes a while to truly understand that you don't have to be macho or mean, that most people don't hook up with tons of girls, that relationships are really mutual, and that everyone is flawed and nervous."

—Male, age twenty-one

Freshmen college students who began drinking or reported being drunk before they were sixteen years of age were more likely than other freshmen to binge drink in college.[9] The restrictions imposed by college administrators can reach only so far on most campuses, where alcohol and drugs are readily available and the hookup scene is widely accepted. The practice of "pregaming" in particular, which students generally engage in out of fear that there will not be enough access to alcohol when they get to a party or a bar, leads to more drinking, high-risk behaviors, and unfavorable consequences such as blackouts, hangovers, unplanned substance abuse, or unprotected sex.[10]

"Some think that drinking alcohol will enhance the experience of physical intimacy when just the opposite is true. Alcohol decreases clitoral sensitivity and vaginal secretions in women and contributes to impotency in men."[11]

—Office of the vice provost for university life
at the University of Pennsylvania

Being a Nondrinker

I grew up in an inn, and observing the drinking habits of guests, friends, and family members had a big impact on me. I decided to be a nondrinker early in my life, even though my siblings insisted I would eventually drink because "all teenagers drink." As a contrary-minded, stubborn kid, I was defiant about my choice. During middle and early high school, I was harshly judgmental of people who drank and did drugs. A friend who was already done drinking and using drugs by tenth grade taught me to accept other people's choices yet stay true to my own conviction to not engage in drugs and alcohol. Because there was no doubt for me, it got easier to enjoy parties and explain my choice if anyone pressured or judged me. By the time I got to college, I had enough practice being sober among drinkers that it didn't take much energy to navigate a serious party culture as a nondrinker.

Cindy's Take

Sometimes I had to pull out some snarl to get into parties as a nondrinker in college. The keg guy at the door would insist that I had to take a beer from him, even though I made it clear I was not interested. When I explained that I didn't drink alcohol, a common response was, "Do you want to hold this beer, so you feel more comfortable at the party?" My snarky response would be, "Do you want me to hold that beer so you feel more comfortable at this party?" I still get this kind of pressure as a middle-aged person. Seventh grade rocks on!

A clear pattern became apparent to me as an adult: in every drinking environment, with all age groups, having a drink in hand puts people at ease, whether it is a first or a tenth drink. In fact, just holding a drink changes people's dispositions: even before they take a sip, they feel more at ease and interact more openly. Today, as a nondrinking innkeeper, I find the tension among guests who arrive early almost unbearable as they try to relax before the alcohol has arrived at the party. Alcohol is a social lubricant on which many people of all ages depend.

Pay attention to your relationship with alcohol as you go through college. Most people assume that by the time college ends, they won't need to depend on alcohol to feel socially comfortable. Unless you consciously make a transition to rely less on alcohol, four years can go by quickly without much change. Many college grads in their twenties and thirties observe that the alcohol-dependent aspect of their friendships from college becomes painfully evident when their post-college gatherings center around heavy alcohol consumption. While these situations help highlight authentic friendships, larger group celebrations may require you to tolerate some inauthentic interactions fueled by alcohol. It is worth keeping a close eye on the evolution of your own social ease, and that of your peers, as you move through college and beyond.

7

Sexual Assault

Knowing the Facts and Advocating for Change

Sexual assault is a complicated crime that can take many forms. As such, it often goes unreported and unaddressed simply because survivors are unsure of whether or not their experience can be considered sexual assault. It is important to understand that there are no strict guidelines on what constitutes sexual assault; the rule of thumb is that if you feel like it was sexual assault, it was. Because sexual assault involves a violation of *your* personal boundaries, *you* are the only one who can say when it has occurred. If you are sexually assaulted:

- Know that what happened was not your fault. Period. End of story.
- Get to a safe place, away from your assailant.
- Reach out to someone you trust. This may be a friend, family member, counselor, medical professional, a person who works at a sexual assault hotline or other organization (see the resources at the back of this book), or anyone else you can count on to provide judgment-free support and guidance. There are many people out there who want to help you. Even if the only thing you know for certain is that you are confused about what happened, know that there are resources to help you figure it out.

- Learn about the resources available to you and what the process will be like if you choose to take medical or legal action, or if you report it to your school.
- Take the course of action that feels right to you.
- One of the most difficult parts of reporting a sexual assault is telling your parents. Most college students don't talk to their parents openly about their sex lives. If the first time you talk to your parents about sex is after you have been assaulted, emotions will be much more intense. Most parents will rise up to be a source of support once they get through the difficulty of accepting the idea that their child has been sexually assaulted.

Sexual Assault Facts

There are a number of basic facts that administrators and students (and the general public) need to get a handle on. Sexual assault is frighteningly common and can have lasting consequences for survivors.

- In 75 to 80 percent of the assaults that occur in college, the survivor knows the attacker before the assault. These perpetrators may be acquaintances, classmates, friends, or past or current significant others.[1]
- Up to 40 percent of survivors acquire a sexually transmitted disease as a result of their rape.[2]
- 6 to 14 percent of college men report committing acts that fall under the legal definition of rape.[3]
- Roughly two-thirds of college repeat rapists are responsible for at least 90 percent of rapes on campuses and average four or more rapes each.
- Eighty percent of rape survivors suffer from chronic physical or psychological conditions related to their assault.[4]

- Rape survivors are thirteen times more likely to attempt suicide than noncrime victims (victims of noncriminal trauma) and six times more likely than victims of other crimes.[5]
- Nineteen percent of undergraduate women reported experiencing attempted or completed sexual assault since entering college in a recent government-funded study.[6] Some studies indicate that the percentage is closer to 25 percent.
- It is not only women who suffer sexual assault. Men are also assaulted, though these cases often go unreported sometimes as a result of social and cultural pressures regarding masculinity. This makes it difficult to get accurate statistics on the incidence of cases with male survivors.
- Although a statistically significant portion of perpetrators are men, women are capable of and do commit sexual assault on others, both men and women.
- The incidence of sexual assault in the LGBTQ community is high; TGQN (transgender, genderqueer, questioning, nonconforming) individuals report a higher incidence of sexual assault than any other group. Transgender individuals are at highest risk, with 64 percent experiencing sexual assault at some point in their lives.[7]
- The incidence of rape by an intimate partner is twice as high for bisexual women as it is for heterosexual women. Approximately one-fifth of bisexual women will experience intimate partner rape, as compared with one-tenth of heterosexual women.[8]
- The Association of American Universities (AAU) conducted a survey of twenty-seven institutions of higher education in the fall of 2014, and found that the 24.1 percent of undergraduate students who identify as TGQN were the most likely to experience sexual assault involving physical force or incapacitation while enrolled in college. Comparatively, 23.1 percent

of female undergraduates and 5.4 percent of male undergraduates had experienced such assaults.[9]

- Though studies specific to college populations are few and have small sample sizes, a synthesis of studies of the experiences of LGBTQ individuals indicates alarmingly high rates of incidence and prevalence in this community. A recent meta-analysis of seventy-five studies examining rates of sexual violence among those who identify as lesbian, gay, or bisexual found that between 16 and 85 percent of lesbian/bisexual women and 12 and 54 percent of gay men survive childhood, adult, intimate partner, and/or hate crime–related sexual assaults in their lifetimes.[10]
- Bisexual women appear to be at the highest risk of being raped, stalked, or subjected to physical violence by an intimate partner among cisgender (non-transgender) individuals; 61 percent experience this during their lifetime. One in three bisexual women have experienced stalking victimization at some point in their lifetime.[11]

David Lisak, a retired associate professor of psychology at the University of Massachusetts, Boston, is considered a leading expert on sexual assault. The research that he and his colleagues have done is compelling and has been confirmed in other studies. Most people are not aware that false reports of sexual assault are significantly lower (2 to 10 percent) than the public perceives, and are equal to the number of false reports for most other crimes. A study conducted by the AAU indicates that about one in four women were sexually assaulted during their time in college.[12] According to RAINN (Rape, Abuse, and Incest National Network), 68 percent of rapes are not reported.[13]

Contrary to most people's assumptions, you cannot recognize the sort of person who might be a rapist because he can be likable, sociable, kind, gentle, and even timid, according to Lisak.[14] Only 10 to 25 percent of rapists are expelled from college. Sexual assaults continue to be underreported, and victims of sexual assault may choose not to report for a number of reasons, including shame, lack of faith in the system, fear of being socially ostracized, fear of revenge, and fear of telling their parents—to name a few.

It is now known that many women who are sexually assaulted do not resist, often because they are overwhelmed by feelings of helplessness and fear of further harm.[15] Survivors have varied responses to being assaulted. Recent research on how trauma impacts the brain and memory reveals that when people experience something very traumatic, the first reaction is to try to undo it or pretend it didn't happen.[16] Often, sexual assault survivors don't show anger initially and act normally toward their rapist, which seems counterintuitive. Aside from experiencing shame, guilt, depression, anger, social problems, alcohol and drug use, and sexual problems, PTSD (post-traumatic stress disorder) rates are high among sexual assault survivors, particularly in the two weeks following the incident. Lisak asserts that self-blame is more common for victims who are raped by an acquaintance. "If you have been assaulted by somebody you thought you could trust," he says, "how do you restore your sense of trust in the world or in people? And how do you trust yourself?"[17]

SEXUAL ASSAULT AND THE BRAIN

Jim Hopper, PhD, is an independent consultant and teacher associate in psychology in the department of psychiatry at Harvard Medical School. He trains investigators, prosecutors, judges, and military commanders on the neurobiology of sexual assault.

In my YouTube presentation "Neurobiology of Trauma and Sexual Assault," I explain how the experience of sexual assault can affect the behaviors and memories of victims in ways that most people still don't understand, including many college administrators and police officers. In short, it's all about the brain's fear circuitry taking over. For example, the prefrontal cortex is the part of our brain that allows us to think rationally and respond rationally. But when the fear circuitry really kicks in, the prefrontal cortex is rapidly impaired by "stress chemicals," and it's not reason but fear-based reflexes and habits that run the show.

Evolution has wired our brains to *freeze* when an attack is first detected. It's an automatic and reflexive response, the fear circuitry sending out a "stop everything" signal to halt current thinking and behavior and focus on assessing the attack and possibilities of escape. Lots of things can happen next, depending on a variety of factors, and they don't all fit into "fight or flight." But they all do tend to be habits and reflexes, not rational responses from the impaired prefrontal cortex. When the fear circuitry assesses escape as impossible or resistance as futile—maybe right away, or after some struggle, or after habitual polite responses to unwanted sexual advances don't work because the attacker won't listen to any form of "no"—the brain may fall back on extreme *survival reflexes*. These include dissociating (blanking out, spacing out, or otherwise disconnecting from the experience, including going on autopilot), tonic immobility (rigid and paralyzed, literally unable to speak or move), or collapsed immobility (limp and paralyzed, faint, "sleepy," or even passed out). What many of these responses have in common is that the victims, for totally brain-based reasons, do not fight or even actively resist the assault—at least not in ways that the victims and others, including their loved ones, believe they *should* have responded, or *would* have responded if it was "really" an assault.

Finally, the terrified brain encodes experiences into memory differently. The fear circuitry focuses attention on what seems essential to survival and coping, on a moment-to-moment basis. And what gets our attention is what gets into memory. The fear circuitry also alters the brain circuitry responsible for encoding into memory those aspects of the experience that do get attention. The result? Many sexual assaults are remembered *not* as complete stories with lots of details in the order they happened, but instead as fragments or islands of memory that can be quite disconnected from each other and difficult or impossible to put into the right order. Such memories are still often misunderstood, unfortunately, as evidence that a victim's memories are too incomplete to be trusted or that she "can't keep her story straight." But such memories are totally consistent with assault and trauma, and some of the pieces they *do* include are recalled vividly and painfully, and are not the things one remembers from a consensual sexual experience.

What if a Friend Is Sexually Assaulted?

If a friend of yours is assaulted, the most valuable thing you can do is tell your friend that you believe, support, and do not judge her or him. Do not try to talk your friend out of it. Be a good listener and ask supportive questions. The reaction of the first person a survivor shares his or her story with can have a major impact on how the person moves forward. Because the process of reporting a sexual assault or sharing the experience with a friend can trigger memories that make the survivor feel retraumatized, it is important to show how much you value the survivor and give the survivor the power to make decisions about how to move forward.[18] Help your friend understand her or his options and the resources available (see the resources section at the end of this book), including professional counseling and support, but remember it is the survivor's decision whether to use them.

Remember that rape is a crime that is about power and control as much as it is about sex, if not more so. This means that if someone you know has experienced sexual assault, it is very possible that person is struggling with the feeling that someone stripped her (or him) of control over her body—and now, in the aftermath, she feels out of control of her emotions, environment, and life. As a supporter, you should do whatever you can to give back to your friend the feeling of control. That means letting her make all the decisions about the healing process herself. You can help the survivor understand the resources and options available, but try not to pressure the person to take any particular type of action. It is her choice. Communicate that your friend has your unequivocal support no matter what she chooses to do.

Protect your friend's privacy; this is obviously a deeply personal matter, and the survivor should have absolute control over who does and does not know about the assault.

Remember also that, no matter what your relationship with the person was like, he (or she) might not want to share anything with you about what happened to him. This does not necessarily have anything to do with you; it is not personal. Allow your friend to dictate the terms of your relationship as he goes through the healing process.

And finally, be aware of how your friend's assault is affecting you. Seek counseling if you need it. There are many resources and support networks available for the friends and families of survivors of assault. Know that if you are struggling emotionally or mentally with what happened to your friend, you might not be the right person to support her or him. If that is the case, be sure to communicate clear boundaries. Though it may feel like you are abandoning your friend, know that it is more helpful in the long run if your friend knows exactly what she can expect from you ahead of time.

How to Be an Advocate at Your School

Education and awareness are the biggest tools in the fight against sexual assault. Get educated and educate your peers. This can be challenging when they are less aware than you would expect or hope. Be patient and focus on the most receptive friends rather than taking on the world, which can leave you drained, disappointed, and angry. It can be particularly frustrating when your good friends don't get it. Trust that you are planting seeds of information that will take root over time.

Many people won't engage with the issue of sexual assault until someone they know has been affected. Part of your work as an advocate is prevention. It is a challenging balance to educate your friends in the hope of minimizing the number who will be affected while those same friends are reluctant to engage in prevention because they aren't yet aware of cases involving people they know personally. The intensity of sexual assault causes some people to actively deny that it is an issue in their community because it is too terrifying. Not everyone will understand the urgency you feel, but keep sharing information with as much patience as you can. To increase your effectiveness, you can also partner with local advocacy organizations and/or volunteer for hotlines.

Welcoming Men to the Change

Unfortunately, many male college students are reluctant to attend events or engage in discussions about sexual assault and consent because they assume that they will be blamed and scolded by the presenter or the women in the audience. And, to be fair, that does sometimes happen. For decades, women's groups have rallied and worked hard to raise awareness about sexual assault, sometimes unintentionally alienating men in the process. But if men are not engaged in the conversation, progress will be slower. While as a woman you might feel defensive and frustrated when you hear the statistics, which implicate men as being responsible for almost all sexual assaults, a lesser-known fact is that 6 to 14 percent of men are responsible for 90 percent of sexual assaults; most college-aged men have not, and will not commit a sexual assault.

Many people generalize about guys and judge them by the groups they hang out with. Often, guys say they have their defenses up before presentations on this topic even begin, because they feel that they are judged by the reputation of their teammates, group of friends, fraternity brothers, or organization. It can be hard for a guy to stay on the high road when he feels that he and his friends are being labeled "the problem." When both women and men are engaged in the conversations about ending sexual violence and creating a safe, healthy community for everyone, we stand a better chance of changing cultural attitudes.

Cindy's Take

The word "privilege" makes a lot of guys feel defensive. When asked what women do to stay safe when they go out at night, guys' hands go up and the guys then generate a long list of ideas. When asked what men do to stay safe when they go out at night, no hands go up. The guys look around, and the room stays silent. This silence reminds us all that it is a privilege for men to not have to worry as much about safety when they go out to a party.

Young men additionally find it frustrating when it's assumed that they fit a hypermasculine stereotype. Demonization of this stereotype makes them feel defensive and conflicted about opening up. Many admit that it is easier to just lay low and hope to avoid being noticed. Thankfully, over the last fifteen years organizations on campuses have begun to welcome men as allies and include male students in conversations, along with female students and administrators. It is extremely important that we continue and expand this practice.

Why We Need to Keep Talking About Affirmative Consent

It is very important for us to continue to make the expectations and language of affirmative consent—clear agreement to engage in sexual activity every step of the way—part of an ongoing conversation that will help us all aim higher. People have been working hard for decades to raise awareness about sexual assault, and there has been dissatisfaction with the slow progress. Activists, survivors, and parents are frustrated that statistics are not improving, that sexual assault is misunderstood by so many, and that cases continue to be mishandled. The tides are turning, however, thanks to persistent conversations about affirmative consent. The documentary film *The Hunting Ground* and Jon Krakauer's book *Missoula* are just two examples featuring personal stories told by courageous survivors that have brought national attention to the issue of campus rape.

Students are being taught to ask for—and wait for—clear, unquestionable consent rather than assuming agreement or risking misinterpretion of nonverbal or verbal cues. Students want and need guidance in navigating the party/hookup scene. Rape is not caused by the amount a person drinks, what a person wears, or a person's inability to read social cues. Rapists cause rape.

What Does Consent Look Like?

Consent is an enthusiastic, verbal "yes!" given by a sober adult who is not under the influence of any form of verbal or physical coercion. The language in the California Senate Bill No. 967, Chapter 748, is quite clear: "Affirmative consent means affirmative, conscious, and voluntary agreement to engage in sexual activity."[19] The following part of the bill is a concept that has only recently gained more widespread understanding: "Affirmative consent must be ongoing throughout a sexual activity and can be revoked at any time."[20] This means both partners check in as the encounter advances to be sure both are comfortable. Silence is not consent. The affirmative consent standard is also described as *enthusiastic consent, positive active consent,* and *yes means yes.* The affirmative consent standard represents a shift on college campuses that encourages students to gain a clearer understanding of what consent looks and sounds like. The more we normalize these phrases and the expectation of affirmative consent, the closer we get to ending sexual assault on campuses. Just in the last year, the shift in attitudes about affirmative consent language, policies, and laws has become more widespread.

Acceptance of the concept of affirmative consent is the first step, and the clear language is having an impact on a large number of young people. Students currently in college are responding positively to affirmative consent practice or are moving in that direction. A surprising number of recent grads talk about how their colleges desperately need changes in their sexual assault policies as well as in the way colleges respond to and punish perpetrators; but many can't fathom communicating in the way affirmative consent laws and policies ask people to do. The common claim that it would be "too awkward" to ask for consent reflects the larger issue that communicating about sex is not easy for people, no matter their age, and is not something we actively teach to young people, though that is changing.

> "I know that as a society we aren't very good about talking openly and honestly about human sexuality and sexual interaction. However, for my definition of what is healthy sexual activity, it necessarily involves that conversation. I tell my students if you can't look someone in the eye and talk about what you want to do with them, you don't have any business doing it."[21]
>
> —Al Vernacchio, author of *For Goodness Sex*

Middle-aged people seem to be the most resistant to the concept of affirmative consent, often projecting their twentieth-century college experiences and perspective onto current college students, who live in a vastly different social landscape. Rather than be exasperated that affirmative consent "turns sex into a checklist" or "takes all the romance away," we need to embrace the positive change and consider that it is not unreasonable to check in, ask if something feels good, and ask, "Is this ok?" Affirmative consent laws and policies will evolve, but their very existence is inspiring positive shifts as school administrators, educators, coaches, parents, and students address consent more directly than ever.

Who Should Ask for Consent?

Getting consent is the responsibility of *both parties* involved in any sexual encounter, regardless of gender. When consent is not obtained during an encounter, it is the fault of the person who did not adequately ask, *not* the person who did not do enough to express a "no." In other words, the fact that a person did not give an unprompted physical or verbal indication of their discomfort with a situation does not make it their "fault" that sexual assault occurred. The guilty party in that situation would be the individual who did not do enough to ensure his or her partner's comfort.

When Should I Get Consent?

You need to ask for consent every single time you engage in sexual activity and all along the way throughout a sexual encounter. Just because you have hooked up with a partner before does not mean that person wants to do so again. Just because you have participated in a certain type of sexual activity before does not mean the person agrees to do it again. Being in a relationship with someone does not give you a magical all-access pass to the person's body; you still need to ask for and receive consent before continuing with any type of sexual activity. This is especially true once drugs and alcohol become involved. Anyone who is intoxicated cannot legally give consent. The same goes for anyone who is asleep or passed out, who cannot understand what is being asked of him or her, or who is a minor.

Verbal Versus Nonverbal Consent

For some reason, a lot of people seem to be under the impression that initiating sex with nonverbal cues is sexier or more romantic. Really, it is just less clear. Sometimes, if you have been in a relationship with someone for a long time, you will get a sense for which nonverbal cues indicate excitement, but even then you may be wrong. With that in mind, it is not possible to appropriately read the nonverbal cues of someone you do not know well, while in a state of optimistic arousal, in the dark, and possibly under the influence of drugs or alcohol. Consider nonverbal cues you are receiving but be alert to whether they match verbal cues; if there's any confusion at all, stop and ask to be sure you and your partner are on the same page.

But It's So Awkward!

I often hear that asking for consent is awkward. What it boils down to is general discomfort with communication around sex. Being partially or fully naked with another person is awkward in itself; therefore, taking that next step into awkwardness by checking in and asking for consent should fit right in. Not being able to look your partner in the eye and ask for consent is a clear indicator that you should not be naked with that person.

It seems that a lot of college students are having sex that doesn't involve a whole lot of communication (or at least honest, active, sober communication). The real secret to better sex is communication. It is worth working on this and getting to the other side of awkward with your partner. Just as every person enjoys different things physically, every person has different boundaries regarding what he or she does, when, and with whom. Getting enthusiastic, affirmative, verbal consent needs to be the first step toward having sex at all. Actively communicating makes sex more fun, comfortable, and pleasurable for both partners.

EASY WAYS TO ASK FOR CONSENT

To make your conversation during a sexual encounter less awkward, yet clear in terms of your partner's consent and comfort level, drop in any (or all) of the following questions:

Do you like this?
Can I do this?

Is this okay?

Does that feel good?

Do you feel comfortable doing _____ right now?

Do you want to _____?

I want to _____. Do you want to do that too, and
    does the timing feel right?

I'd like to do _____. Do you want to, and if not, what
    would you like to do?

Alcohol and Sexual Assault

Bucknell University psychologist William Flack conducted a study of hookup culture in 2001, at the suggestion of his students. According to his research, both women and men said 77.8 percent of unwanted sex happened in a hookup (compared with 13.9 percent that occurred in a relationship and 8.3 percent on a date). Flack says, "It's safe to say that when you are looking at sexual assault, hooking up is a significant risk factor."[22]

When parents hear about sexual assaults, binge drinking, and incidents of students being intubated at the hospital after blacking out from alcohol, they tend to use fear in their last-minute attempts to prepare their kids for college. Generally, these last-ditch efforts are ineffective. Young men receive harsh warnings from their parents that their lives will be ruined if they commit sexual assault. However, young men may have difficulty reconciling those messages with the realities of the college party scene, where heavy drinking and capitalizing on hookup opportunities are part of the culture.

The process of creating a culture of affirmative consent on college campuses is in motion. Bystander programs are empowering students to intervene when they see friends at risk of committing or being vulnerable to sexual assault, as well as to speak up when peers are disrespectful online and off. For decades, we have warned young women that they can avoid being raped if they don't drink too much, stay with friends at parties, and avoid dressing seductively. Aside from blaming the victims for the way they dress and how much they drink, these guidelines have not worked to reduce sexual assault because that approach doesn't change the mindset of the perpetrators or contribute to creating consent culture in a community.

The high rate of sexual assault, including a large number of unreported sexual assaults, indicates that more comprehensive alcohol, sexuality, and consent education for both boys and girls, starting in late elementary school and continuing through high school and college, would help young people better navigate the college party scene. Particularly when kids are raised in a restrictive environment, it is unfair to expect them to automatically gain self-restraint with regard to sex and alcohol once they reach college, especially when alcohol is viewed as an acceptable way to reduce inhibition and a means to avoid taking responsibility. Those of you who have the opportunity to make choices, stumble, face consequences, and take responsibility for your behaviors when you are kids will stand a better chance of making healthier decisions when you are on your own.

WORDS FROM A COUNSELOR

Following are comments from a college sexual assault counselor, speaking about the cultural and campus trends she has witnessed regarding sexual assault.

I'm sincerely concerned about victim blaming. Sexual misconduct is wrong in all forms, and efforts to change the culture around sexual expectations, power and control, and communication among partners are vital to a safe and healthy society. However, cultural change does not happen overnight and until it occurs, people who rely on it as a strategy for well-being may experience avoidable harm. Sexual assault is a life-changing, devastating event. Once it is done, there is no going back. The wound festers; the scars remain; all aspects of life must be reorganized to manage the effects of trauma. There is no energy to advocate for culture change, only pain and focused efforts to heal.

Along with culture change and many, many efforts to teach healthy sexuality, let's empower people to actively lower their risk. Anyone who drinks alcohol or chooses to engage in hookups has a right to know that statistically, these are high-risk situations that are more likely to result in harm than their alternatives. It doesn't imply that you can't or shouldn't. It does require, as a favor to one's future well-being, a heightened awareness of warning signs, to step out of the way of an assault should one come your way. Drink less, don't walk alone at night, watch your drink, require that your partners provide consent you clearly understand and that they respect your boundaries at the first ask . . . not because you grant permission for someone to harm, but because you have no tolerance for harm in even its infancy. Shine light on anything and everything that smacks of risk as a means to create a culture free of sexual violence.

The Move Toward Transparency

Upholding the school's reputation and encouraging alumni giving are just two of the reasons schools have been motivated to keep sexual assault cases on their campuses out of the limelight. We have reached a point where colleges that mishandle cases and prevent them from moving forward will fall under harsh scrutiny, and colleges and universities are changing their policies and processes.

Those schools with the courage to be fully transparent with reports of sexual assault, allow for due process, and discipline perpetrators appropriately will ultimately prevail, drawing more alumni support and competitive applicants over time.

Hope for Change

Many colleges have groups of students—such as Women's Forum, Men's Forum, MAASV (Male Athletes Against Sexual Violence), MVP (Mentors for Violence Protections), MAV (Men Against Violence), Men of Strength, Respect Works, and Party With Consent—that work to fight sexual violence on campus. I have a number of student mentors who are current leaders of college organizations or have continued the work since graduation. It is from these young people that I first learned about enthusiastic consent, yes means yes, and affirmative consent. Many of these students are in charge of finding and choosing speakers and performers who can bring a different perspective to campus.

Recently, I spoke at Cedar Crest College, where I met a young woman who is a student leader. She had done a research project about an app used to report and record the details of a sexual assault anonymously. The app was designed to give users the opportunity to formally report a sexual assault or to record the details anonymously and decide whether to proceed with a formal report later. One can record an experience in the system while the details are fresh, yet remain anonymous, and if the same perpetrator assaults another person, the anonymous survivor will be notified. This could motivate the person to come forward, because she or he no longer feels alone and is inspired to stop the perpetrator from assaulting anyone else. When students are engaged in changing the culture on their campus, the student climate becomes much more socially healthy.

What Colleges Are Doing

Colleges are engaging students with presentations and workshops focused on sexual assault, binge drinking, hookup culture, bystander behavior, consent culture, and the ways messages in marketing and media contribute to these issues. Films such as *The Hunting Ground* are being shown on campuses across the country, and professors are engaging students in class discussions, connecting their subject area to affirmative consent laws and policies. Coaches, advisors, and administrators are creating opportunities to educate students about sexual assault and affirmative consent. Information is distributed through social media as well as through posters and mass e-mails. Almost all new student orientation programs include presentations, training, and workshops about sexual assault and consent using a wide variety of approaches. Most schools offer a lot of great programming, though getting students to attend can be a challenge.

The programs are making an impact, and more are being implemented with younger students each year. Current college sophomores, for instance, are more aware than current seniors by virtue of having participated in more bystander behavior and consent programming in middle and high school. Awareness education is a big part of the solution. Following are examples of some programs that have had success. The Date Safe Project and Speak About It are two popular and impactful programs. The Prevention Intervention Research Center (PIRC) has two evidence-based prevention strategies: the Bringing in the Bystander In-Person Prevention Program and the Know Your Power Bystander Social Marketing Campaign. Detailed descriptions of these programs are included in the resource section beginning on page 169.

Signs of the Changing Culture

We are witnessing an orchestrated cultural shift that makes it more common for young people to check in with their partners throughout a sexual encounter. The idea of asking for consent throughout a sexual experience becomes a more realistic expectation as the language is normalized. Some students admit that they aren't there yet, but they are working on it. I have heard a few young men say they have avoided asking for consent because they fear being rejected, but recognize that this is a risk. Their solution had been to tread carefully, looking for what they considered a balance: a partner who didn't say no and seemed receptive. Many now understand that guessing that a partner "seems" receptive puts them at risk for committing sexual assault. We need to keep the dialogue going and refine our approaches for changing attitudes. That said, the comments of students like those below reflect the positive changes occurring on campuses.

"More guys are asking for consent and saying things like, 'Let me know if this makes you uncomfortable' on the dance floor *and* in the bedroom. At parties, members of the host fraternity check in with someone who is in a risky situation or even if something seems off between two people. It is way more accepted for hosts of parties to watch out for people and speak up to ensure their safety. People know there are lists with names and numbers of guys in leadership roles around the house and encourage people to contact them if they have an issue."

—Male, age twenty-two

"Recently, I've been asked for consent much more clearly and more often. I think more sexual assault resources have become prominent, and the student wellness center has done a lot to become more known. I think the key thing that caused men to care about the issue were when big, public cases about sexual assaults involving students on our campus who went to trial and everyone knew about it. Hearing about the outcomes of those was a huge deal and made people realize the issue was real."

—Female, age twenty-one

A number of factors have, in recent years, produced a surge in efforts to create a culture of consent on college campuses. In addition to some high-profile sexual assault cases reported in the media, the frustration among survivors of sexual assault and advocates for change reached a tipping point. In January of 2013, Annie E. Clark and Andrea Pino (who were featured in the documentary *The Hunting Ground*), along with three other students at the University of North Carolina at Chapel Hill, filed federal Title IX and Clery complaints against UNC with the U.S. Department of Education. Their case led to investigations of how colleges and universities nationwide handle sexual assault cases, including violations of Title IX relating to sexual assault. Their case helped make sexual assault prevention and fair treatment of survivors a priority both on campuses and in our wider society. The Campus Sexual Assault Victims' Bill of Rights (also called the Clery Act) requires that colleges and universities annually disclose a summary of a policy specifically addressing three main areas of sexual assault, including victims' rights, disciplinary procedures, and educational programming. Noncompliant colleges and universities can be fined up to $35,000 or lose their eligibility to participate in federal student aid programs.

Clark and Pino, together with Sofie Karasek, cofounded End Rape on Campus (EROC) with a mission to end campus sexual violence through direct support for survivors and their communities; prevention through education; and policy reform at the campus, local, state, and federal levels (check out EROC at endrapeoncampus.org). Thanks to the work of EROC and other organizations, more college students have an understanding of affirmative consent. Most college campuses are aiming to create a culture of consent by way of increased educational programming. Intervention is becoming a more accepted and normal practice among students at parties on many college campuses. Progress is in motion. Please check out the resource section at the end of this book, where you can review sexual assault resources and terms and learn more about effective programs to bring to your campus.

8

LGBTQ

Getting Informed and Showing Respect

Most college students have heard about the concept of sexuality and gender as existing on spectrums, but many are confused about what exactly that means, how it works, and how they can talk about it without accidentally being offensive. I have been lucky enough to have friends who are experts on gender and sexual identities and are professional speakers on the topic. Fortunately, they have been patient with me over the years and have helped me understand the issues. I am going to pass along their valuable teachings here.

"Fluid" in terms of sexuality and gender is the best way to properly describe the way many people self-identify. The concept of a "fluid spectrum" refers to the increasingly accepted idea that, rather than existing within the binary of "male" or "female" and "straight" or "gay," the majority of people are actually more accurately described as being somewhere along the line between these poles. An individual's position on this spectrum can change, both over the course of his or her lifetime and day to day. As one person wrote to me in an e-mail:

> My sexual attractions, behaviors, and identities have changed over the years, and it's not because I've been confused and struggling to understand the "Real Me." It is because I'm

sexually fluid. This is not a phase! Sexual fluidity, essentially, is the notion that, like many other things in the world, sexuality isn't fixed. It isn't "This is what it is, and this is what it will be, forever and ever and ever." It's the idea that, hey, things change—and that we can allow them to.

People may feel very strongly that they are male or female, or may feel somewhere in the middle. They might be attracted to one gender, both genders, or not feel sexual attraction to anyone at all! Please remember that the feelings of attraction that others are experiencing are every bit as strong and real as whatever form of sexual attraction you yourself experience. Also remember that, just as you probably don't want to be asked in detail about your sexual proclivities (no one, after all, has the *right* to know anything about your sexual interests), others are in no way obligated to explain their choices and attractions to you.

You may not always be sure of the sexual orientation and gender identity of those around you, and it may not be necessary for you to know. Set aside your curiosity out of respect for people. It is possible that the person is genderqueer—doesn't identify as male or female—and would rather not discuss their gender identity. It is usually appropriate to ask a person how they identify if you need to address them and want to avoid making assumptions that may be offensive or hurtful. As long as you ask politely, with respectful intentions, how a person identifies, your question will generally be well received. I understand that this vocabulary can still be pretty confusing, though; some terms and their definitions can be found in the helpful glossary at the end of this book.

Heterosexual describes what our culture assumes to be the most accepted relationship, a woman and a man. This assumption is heteronormative—making heterosexuality an identity and an expected behavior of the privileged group. Relationships can vary in a number of ways, as can gender and sex. It is our responsibility to educate ourselves and listen to other people as they share their stories and ways of identifying. Whether another person's story is reflected in our own lives isn't the point. Being able to listen, perceive, and validate another's story is truly being an ally.

—Jessica Pettitt, speaker and consultant,
GoodEnoughNow.com

The Role of Cultural Gender Stereotypes

Acceptance of the concepts of sexual and gender fluidity is tremendously influenced by widespread gender stereotypes. It is frequently noted that bisexuality is "believed" more when it is seen in women; according to Jane Ward, associate professor of gender and sexuality studies at the University of California, Riverside, "Straight women are also given considerable leeway to have occasional sexual contact with women without the presumption that they are actually lesbians. In other words, same-sex contact among straight men and women is interpreted through the lens of some well-worn gender stereotypes."[1] Bisexuality is not the same as sexual fluidity, of course, but this quotation aptly describes a societal standard that equally applies to the way we treat individuals as they discover where they land or how they move on the spectrum of sexual attraction.

Widespread commodification of women reduces them to objects of sexual desire—generally, heterosexual male sexual desire—and this seems to have made people loath to believe that a woman's sexuality does not include a desire for heterosexual sex. They are more than willing to believe that she wants to have sex with men, and often dismiss any sexual relations that she may have had with other women or nonbinary individuals as "phases." Worse still, women engaging in nonheterosexual sex are often appropriated as further fodder for the male sexual appetite. "Girl-on-girl" is a popular form of pornography, for example, that serves to convert the act of a woman having sex with another woman into an object of male desire.

The judgment described above contributes to denying men sexual agency in a similar way. Rather than allowing them the freedom to explore their sexuality, it transforms experimentation into choice. They cannot explore relations with other men (or nonbinary individuals) without being forever categorized as "not straight." Many women say they would have a difficult time believing that a man was interested in women at all if they heard that he had once had sex with a man. Whereas with women we are, as a society, perhaps too eager to think of women as straight, we are absolutely unwilling to allow men room for sexual experimentation.[2]

The reality is that sexual experimentation is a normal part of learning to understand yourself, and this is true for everyone. You should feel free and comfortable pursuing any individual whom you find sexually attractive (as long as you do so in a respectful and consensual way). I hope that you also feel comfortable *not* engaging in sex with any partner if you don't want to. There is an absurd amount of pressure in our culture for young people to be having sex; the notion that you need to engage in sexual activity to prove you are sexually empowered is absurd. Remember that a key part of sexual freedom is the freedom to choose whether or not to engage in sex at all. A lot of college students think that they are "the only ones" not having sex, but a recent study of undergraduate students published in *New York* magazine reported that 39 percent of the students they interviewed were virgins.[3]

THE PROGRAM ON INTERGROUP RELATIONS

Conversations about differences can be challenging among diverse groups of students on campuses. Issues such as race, gender identity, sexual orientation, and gender equality can potentially create discord on campuses with students who vocalize prejudices or intolerance. Some students are eager to learn about others and are open to change despite being brought up in an intolerant environment; however, fear of offending others and a lack of comfort entering into a conversation about differences can keep people divided. As campuses have grown more diverse, new programs have been implemented to educate students and to facilitate conversations among students, faculty, and administrators.

Mike Wooten is a senior assistant dean of residential life and director of residential educational at Dartmouth College. While at the University of Michigan, Wooten taught in the university's Program on Intergroup Relations (IGR), which blends theory and experiential learning to facilitate students' learning about social group identity, social inequality, and intergroup relations.[4] The Program on Intergroup Relations is a nationally recognized academic social justice program that originated at the University of Michigan in 1988 as a means of addressing racial tension.[5]

Wooten explained a new initiative at Dartmouth: first-year students on each floor will stay together all their years on campus, moving as a unit within a cluster of dorms. The intention is to extend orientation by facilitating dialogue and intentionally create community. Along with undergraduate assistants (UGAs) living on each floor, the reimagined house communities will have a faculty and graduate student presence, as well as a community director who works to administer the entire program. Group dinners, presentations by guests speakers, and discussions provide opportunities to teach dialogue skills. The new House Communities open in fall of 2016, combining the best of the college's previous residential program models and peer best practices.

High Stress for Nonconforming Students

Feeling marginalized, unsupported, and misunderstood are just a few of the reasons gender-nonconforming students experience higher rates of stress and anxiety. According to *Safe & Respected*, a guide published by New York City's Administration for Children's Services, LGBTQ (lesbian, gay, bisexual, transgender, questioning or queer) young people are two to five times more likely than their heterosexual peers to report skipping school because they have felt isolated or experienced violence. LGBTQ youth are more than four times as likely to have felt unsafe during the past month and to have made a serious suicide attempt in the past year.

> "My initial impression has been that our campus is far more hetero-normative, cisnormative, and party focused than I had hoped. On the one hand, that is true everywhere. I would like to see our campus become a community in which it is okay to be LGBTQ and out because I have heard from other queer students that they felt like they had to go back into the closet when they got here, which is truly sad and not at all what this school purports to be."
>
> —First-year college student

According to Lee Che Leong, director of the Teen Health Initiative at the NYCLU, "Curricular inclusion, especially within health education models, is a necessary component of remedying the isolation of LGBTQ youth."[6] One potential factor in higher suicide rates in LGBTQ youth is that stigma and prejudice exist at an institutional level, including within schools, mental health and social services, and health care services.[7] Training educators and providers is crucial to support and protect LGBTQ youth. In one study, college students who reported "cross-gender roles"—having gender traits or expressions more often associated with the other sex—were at higher risk for suicidal symptoms, regardless of their sexual orientation.[8]

BEING A TRANS-INCLUSIVE INSTITUTION

Loren Cannon, Humboldt State University, Department of Philosophy

As a faculty member who wishes to respect all of my students and their complex collection of identities and histories, hearing that any student feels that they are dealing with institutional injustice on campus is significant and often a catalyst for deep reflection on my own behavior. Additionally, the fact that I am trans, have personally experienced being the only transgender student in the classroom, and am one of few trans faculty and staff members makes the experiences of injustice resonate very close to home. I thought I'd take a moment to explain some of my thoughts on what it means to be a trans-inclusive institution and how faculty members can support trans students in the classroom setting.

Back in 2007, I was invited to the office of our university's former president to discuss the realities of being trans in the workplace and how to serve trans-identified students. The invitation was due to the change of HSU's nondiscrimination policy that included prohibition of discrimination against individuals on the basis of gender identity or gender expression. I applauded this change of the policy, but honestly, was not sure that he (or others) knew what it would entail. Since that time there have been numerous conversations, trainings, and initiatives on the topic of how to serve all our students, including those who identify as trans, more equitably.

As a trans student, I remember waiting outside my professor's office to discuss how he was misgendering me every day in class. Each time he used the wrong pronoun, there would be the sound of collective inhalation as the students in the class noticed his error and then waited to see how I would react. I tried to ignore it and continue articulating my question or comment, but it was very difficult for me. I hated both being misgendered and being the center of attention as all the other students watched how I would handle this intensely awkward and embarrassing moment. I felt terribly alone. When I spoke to him in his office, I was a sweaty, voice-trembling, nervous wreck. Still, somehow I said what was needed and things improved. While my professor had some knowledge that trans persons existed, he was astounded that one such as myself was actually a student on campus.

These experiences, and discussions with other trans persons, lead me to believe that, generally, being called something other than one's preferred pronoun and preferred name can cause significant harm. To intentionally or thoughtlessly misgender someone or refer to them with a name other than their preferred one is disrespectful. Sometimes it can make a person feel invisible (or, alternatively, too visible), or that the only part of one's life that gets attention is exactly that aspect of one's history that is being intentionally put aside. Sometimes it can feel like there is no refuge in a world that ignores personal attempts at self-respect and self-actualization. According to a study conducted by the Gay, Lesbian, and Straight Education Network (GLSEN) nearly all trans students are verbally harassed and more than half are physically assaulted.[9] Trans students experience particularly hostile high school climates that make it difficult to stay in high school, let alone persevere to the college level. Nearly all studies that attempt to describe the experience of trans persons report that being white and having other privileges does, predictably and unjustly, make things easier. I believe this is true of my own story. Being trans inclusive means that we recognize, as an institution, that not all trans persons have the same experiences, histories, identifications, and privileges.

I believe that being trans inclusive means empowering all students to designate their preferred name on class rosters, Moodle [education software], and the like. Software technology is here to serve us, not to make persons of certain groups vulnerable to intentional and unintentional harm. Until these software problems are solved, (we) faculty members can adopt practices that respect trans students without putting the onus on them to, *semester after semester*, approach us to ask us to make an exception to our usual practice. I believe that being a campus that values the diverse identities and histories of our students does not mean that we treat certain students as exceptions to the rule, but adopt practices that serve all students equitably. Using a sign-in sheet is a good alternative to calling roll, as is asking students to fill out notecards and identify their preferred name and pronoun. (Simply Googling "Serving Trans Students Equitably" will provide lots of handy tips.) This practice is respectful for trans students and the hundreds of others that would rather go by "Hank" than "Henry," "TJ" rather than "Tabatha-Jo," or "Brenda" instead of "Aaron." It is no concern of mine what name a student wishes to be referred by, and this is true of trans as well as cisgender (not transgender) students. I want to learn the name that supports their identity and their learning, not one that brings to the foreground negative memories or, worse yet, "outs" them and puts them at emotional and physical risk.

Lastly, perhaps it should be noted that knowing another's choice of pronoun or name is not an invitation to critique these most personal choices. Being trans inclusive means being supportive of these decisions by others even if they don't coincide with one's own expectations. No one is obligated to approximate another's image of a "Frank," a "Francine," a "Chris," or any other name, whether it seems quite gendered or gender neutral. Similarly with pronouns, one is not obligated to choose one that passes some sort of critique by certain others. Identifying oneself by a chosen name and pronoun is one of the most revolutionary and personally significant events of one's life, and one that often is arrived at only after much personal reflection. In my view, being trans inclusive is respecting another's identity regardless of one's own perception, preconceived notions, and comfort.

"Administrators and students alike may feel discomfort with frankly discussing LGBT sexuality, which undoubtedly contributes to the marginalization of LGBT survivors' experiences. As a result of invisibility, LGBT students may be more vulnerable to experiencing sexual violence. Education and awareness about LGBT sexual violence should be part of a comprehensive program that provides accurate and nonjudgmental education about LGBT sexualities, and should be balanced with positive messages about consent, choice, and the fundamental human right of all to a safe, inclusive, and healthy campus sexual culture."

—Susan Marine, PhD, assistant professor and program director, higher education program, Merrimack College

Calling People Out for Disrespectful Language

It is important to address casual use of disrespectful language with your peers, including use of words that are commonly heard and may not seem hateful to you. Use of words such as "gay" or "fag" is something you need to address directly and in the moment with peers. Regardless of how the words are intended, they have power all their own. I have heard people say, "I would *never* say those words to my gay friends! That would be disrespectful," as if this restraint reflects the ultimate act of inclusivity and respect. The ability to select your audience is evidence enough that you know better. Using terms like "tranny" or "he/she" is considered disrespectful and unacceptable.

Even in college, many of your peers are questioning their gender or sexual identity or are not ready to come out. By using disrespectful language, you send a message to people around you that you may not be a supportive and accepting friend. Sometimes people use homophobic language intentionally to convince peers that they are not gay or to cover the fact that they are gay or questioning. At other times, these words are used out of laziness or even to signal that you are not comfortable having an openly gay friend. Call each other out, and accept being called out if you utter these words.

Cindy's Take

Pronouns are simpler than we make them out to be. Individuals decide on the pronoun they would like to use. The grammar police have expanded their rules to accept "they," "them," and "their" for genderqueer people who don't fall into the binary of "he" or "she." Rise up and step into a respectful, open mindset. If you don't know what pronoun to use, ask in a respectful manner.

REFUSING TO LIVE A LIE

Andrew Goldstein is a research scientist, public speaker, and antibullying advocate. A three-time All-Ivy League and two-time NCAA Division/All-American honoree lacrosse goaltender at Dartmouth College, Andrew came out to his team after his sophomore season. After graduating, Andrew became the first openly gay man in the U.S. to be drafted into a professional sports team, playing for the Boston Cannons and the Long Island Lizards. He has been actively involved with the You Can Play Project and in 2015 cofounded the Courage Game to encourage and support gay youth, rebuke bullying, and promote wider education and awareness for LGBT equality in sports. Following is Andrew's experience.

When I was being recruited to play lacrosse in college, there wasn't a single example of an openly gay athlete on any college or professional team. I heard my teammates say things like, "Stop being a fag," "That's so gay," and "Let's beat those homos" on a daily basis, and it suggested to me that I would never be accepted as my true self. It kept me constantly in fear of being found out. I did everything I possibly could to project the image of a heterosexual athlete, which everyone assumed I was, including dating girls, just to make sure my friends and teammates saw me as straight. It was exhausting to live a lie.

As I got older, it became more difficult to deny who I was and to date people I wasn't romantically interested in. I began dating my first boyfriend in secret during my sophomore season, the same season I became a leader on the field and was named All-New England, All-Ivy League, All-American, and team MVP. My success on the field gave me the confidence to share my truth with my teammates. I didn't want to hold it inside anymore. I thought, "They can't kick their MVP off the team." I was right.

My teammates were surprised but they supported me. Many of my teammates apologized for the things they had said in the past, realizing it must have been awful to hear gay slurs from them and then have to go out and practice or play together. Had I known that my teammates would accept and support me in the way they did, I certainly would not have spent as many sleepless nights in fear of being found out or attempted to date girls simply to mislead my teammates.

On a team, you just want every athlete to be at his best, and this starts with everyone feeling safe to be himself. My teammates stopped using homophobic language in the locker room, and eventually I felt comfortable bringing my boyfriend to the postgame reception alongside my teammates' girlfriends. We were all able to simply be athletes and play together. It is not surprising that those years, when my teammates rallied around me and showed that everyone is welcome as long as he does his job on the field, were some of the best seasons in the history of our school's program. After coming out and being supported by my teammates, I won All-Ivy League and All-American again as an openly gay athlete. I wish I could go back and show my younger self that it's okay to be himself, that he can achieve success on the field, respect in the locker room, and be gay.

Before coming out, most people who are in the closet have known for some time that they are gay, whether it has been weeks, months, years, or decades. It's important to remember that when they decide to tell a friend, family member, teammate, coach, or anyone else, that person has just seconds to respond. Sometimes that person may have suspected that it would eventually play out like this, but often he is hearing news that changes the version of life he has imagined. Not everyone will respond perfectly, and we shouldn't put pressure on that person to say, "I love you no matter what. You're still the same person to me." It may take the person some time to catch up to this news. Sometimes parents have to mourn the death of the vision of life they have in their head for their child. Sometimes a friend has to get upset and wonder why he wasn't told this news earlier, why he was lied to for so long.

I would advise anyone coming out to give his or her loved ones the necessary time to process and to trust that they will eventually come around and realize that they love you no matter what and that you are still the same person. This is especially true today, when you can legally get married, have children, and live a happy life like anyone else. Sometimes you can control when you come out and do it in a strategic manner, when you feel safe, strong, and supported regardless of the response you get. Some people are accidentally outed when they haven't prepared to share the news. Regardless of how it happens, remember to be patient and give yourself and others time to work it out.

If you suspect someone you know might be gay and is keeping it from you, it is unlikely he or she will respond well if confronted about it. Instead, try these three steps: (1) Let the person know that you are there for him if he ever has anything he wants to talk about. (2) Make it clear that you are an ally and would support friends or teammates who are gay. (3) Do what you can to keep the environment free of homophobic slurs. If you truly believe your teammate or friend may be gay, taking these steps will make his life easier and he will appreciate what you have done for him more than you will ever know. It is not our responsibility to push closeted friends or teammates to come out. There are a number of reasons that someone may be hiding it, including the fear of being rejected or being seen as different, or perhaps the person may not be ready to admit it to himself. I don't know whether I would have come out earlier if my teammates had taken these steps, but it would have made me feel supported and allowed me to live without fear.

If there is one thing we could do as a society that would make it easier for LGBT youth, particularly athletes, it would be to stop making the assumption that everyone is straight. We use homophobic language without thinking about who might be hurt. We ask, "Do you have a girlfriend yet?" assuming that every male athlete wants to date girls. When we make these assumptions, it plays out in really small ways that build up over time and make anyone who feels different believe he will never be accepted for who he truly is. In fact, Caitlyn Jenner was once considered the greatest male athlete on the planet, and it turns out that she was doing everything she could to project the manliest image possible while she felt like a woman inside. If we take that extra second to think about what we say, to let go of our assumptions about people and try to be as inclusive as possible, we can make the lives of our friends and teammates dramatically better. In the team environment, that could be the difference between winning and losing.

Parents Need Training and Information Too

Your parents' generation is more open and comfortable supporting LGBTQ kids than their parents' generation. While there has been progress, it can take years for kids to get up the courage to come out to their parents, for a multitude of reasons. If parents have made derogatory comments about LGBTQ people, their kids may delay coming out and avoid the conversation or talk to someone else who is more supportive. The biggest risk is that these kids may suffer emotionally because they are concealing their true selves, fearing rejection or abandonment by family or friends. This increases their risk for physical and emotional health issues.

Out of a fear that intolerant people will direct injurious homophobic, transphobic, or biphobic actions toward their child, well-intentioned parents sometimes make unsupportive, ignorant comments to a child who decides to come out. After wrestling with their own assumptions and fears, some parents are able to give their unconditional love and support to their son or daughter. Because cruelty and lack of acceptance in pockets of our society could make life challenging for their kid, parents can be irrationally concerned at first. Educating parents to help them understand may require patience. Some need to hear how ineffective it is for people to undergo sexual orientation change effort (SOCE), therapies also known as "conversion therapy," "reparative therapy," and "reorientation therapy." These "therapies," instead of changing a person's orientation, may push many back into the closet and contribute to mental health issues. As college students living in a diverse population, you are a trustworthy source to help your parents' generation get beyond their heteronormative view and realize that people they know, work with, or share a community with may identify differently. Talk to your parents about how tolerance and acceptance would reduce the mental health challenges that so many young people suffer while trying to mask their sexual or gender identity.

"I came to campus as a super-closeted person and am now somewhere in the middle of being attracted to men and women depending on the person. Luckily, it was the norm to be gay or at least joke about it amongst my friend group. However, sexual identity is much less free and fluid on campus. Most people refer to me as a lesbian, which is fine. I get the sense that a lot of people are scared of labels, which is a big factor in their carefully calculated experimentation. Maybe it's also partly because the gay community is nonexistent unless you are a super gay, in which case it's kind of exclusive and defining."

—Female, age twenty-one

Most students would like to be considered respectful and inclusive members of their college community. Members of the LGBTQ community continue to be marginalized on many college campuses, despite efforts to educate students and faculty about inclusion. College is a time when students have an opportunity to develop a deeper capacity to accept and understand differences. Reading the glossary of terms and definitions included at the end of this book can be a step toward broadening your awareness and understanding of accepted terminology for people in the LGBTQ community. Engaging in programs and attending presentations will make you more aware of the personal and political aspects of the challenges faced by LGBTQ people. Recently, a broader range of perspectives from the LGBTQ community has been written and become more widely available. Jackson Wright Shultz is a scholar and activist who recorded the stories of more than thirty people who identify as transgender in his book *Trans/Portraits: Voices from Transgender Communities*. Expose yourself to educational resources and contribute to making your campus a more welcoming place by spreading awareness and respect in your community.

9

Safer Sex

What You Need to Know About STIs and Contraception

Protecting yourself from sexually transmitted infections (STIs) and avoiding pregnancy, if and when you decide to be sexually active with a partner, are a critical part of being a responsible adult. Talking to your partner about preventing pregnancy and protecting yourselves from STIs takes courage. (The medical community is increasingly tending toward the use of "STI" in sexual health literature, in an effort to clarify that not every sexually transmitted infection will progress to a disease.) Some people are concerned about how to respond to a partner who may resist using protection or birth control. Having prepared responses can help you make it clear that you won't have sex without contraception or protection. You may find it particularly challenging to hold your boundaries in the heat of the moment—always bring the conversation back to making health a priority. This also means you need to be ready to *not* have sex if your partner pressures you to compromise your values.

If you are comfortable enough to engage in sexual activity with a partner, you should hold yourself to a standard of courage and be able to discuss birth control methods and ask if your partner has been tested for STIs. Nearly 40 percent of people report that they did not use a condom during their last sexual experience and didn't have a conversation about it.[1] These conversations are awkward because having sex is awkward. Once you endure the awkwardness a couple of times, you will find that you can get to the other side of awkward. It will be easier to have these conversations each time, and eventually broaching the subject will become a habit. Discomfort should be a signal to pause and reconsider your choice to engage in sex with that person at all. Planning and effort are required to use contraception correctly and ensure you are as safe as possible. Here are some suggestions to help you hold your ground. For some of these questions or statements, the words "dental dam" or "contraception" can work in place of the word condom:

Statement: I didn't bring a condom.
Response: I have one in my backpack.

Statement: But you are on the pill (or have an IUD or NuvaRing).
Response: That doesn't protect us from STIs.

Question: Can't we have sex without a condom just this once?
Response: Once is all it takes to get pregnant or contract an STI.

Question: Do you think I have an STI?
Response: Some people aren't aware that they have an STI.

Question: Don't you trust me?
Response: It is not about trust. I care about you enough to want us both to be safe.

Statement: I don't like using condoms.
Response: I don't like taking risks.

Statement: I can't get off when I use a condom.
Response: I can't relax without using one, so I guess we won't have sex.

Statement: Condoms feel strange.
Response: STIs are much worse.

Statement: These condoms don't feel right.
Response: Let's try a different brand.

Statement: I don't know how to put on a condom.
Response: I will help.

Statement: It doesn't feel that sexy to wear a condom.
Response: Getting pregnant or an STD doesn't feel that sexy to me.

*Statement: You must not love me enough if you won't have sex with
    me without a condom.*
Response: I love you enough that I won't risk your health or mine.

Statement: I will pull out before I ejaculate.
Response: That is too risky and not reliable enough for me.

Condoms are your best bet to avoid contracting an STI. While not
dependable for preventing pregnancy on their own, condoms also
reduce the chance of getting pregnant. "Safe sex" is not entirely possible because condoms are not 100 percent effective; they do, however, make sex *safer*. Using condoms correctly and consistently is not
as common as we would like to believe, despite the claims of many
college students. Sober students insist they use condoms "all the
time"; however, the health services professionals on campuses across
the country report that they treat a high number of STIs and listen to students' regrets about their heat-of-the-moment or drunken
decision to have sex without a condom. It is not uncommon to hear
about students being treated for yeast infections in the anus, chlamydia or gonorrhea in the throat, or herpes lesions/cold sores on

genitals or the mouth area. Condoms are your best bet for protecting yourself from these and other STIs (even if condoms cannot protect you from the emotional risks surrounding sexual encounters).

There are a number of reasons college students don't use condoms even if they have them on hand and fully intend to use them. Some guys claim that it can be hard to get it up or get off using a condom, particularly when they are drunk or get distracted. Some women decide that because they are on the pill or have a vaginal ring, they feel comfortable foregoing the use of a condom. Some guys brag that they must be too big for condoms because they break several during a hookup. I want to make it very clear that most condom breakage is not related to penis size, since most regular-sized condoms can fit over an adult's forearm up to the elbow. It is more likely that condoms break when penetration is done in a pounding, jackhammer style (as seen in a large percentage of porn), especially when his partner is not aroused and/or lubricated. The combination of dryness and friction can shred condoms.

Menstrual cramps and irregular periods are common reasons parents agree that their daughter should use a birth control method like the pill or the vaginal ring, which release hormones known to reduce the side effects of menstruation. Parents often feel relieved to not have to think about being grandparents any time soon, and send their daughters off to college with a prescription for birth control pills, the patch, shots, an implant, or a vaginal ring. These forms of birth control are effective in preventing pregnancy when used correctly, but many young women who use these methods contract or pass along STIs when they choose to have sex without a condom. Condoms should be used regardless of what other method is in place. Students should make sure they have access to condoms just in case.

Abstinence is the most reliable way to avoid pregnancy or STIs, but it is unrealistic to expect this for many college students. If you are in a monogamous relationship and you both get tested, it is unlikely you will contract an STI. The hookup culture that has normalized casual sex with multiple partners and doesn't demand condom use puts people at risk for contracting an STI.

> "According to Stanford University's Sexual Health Peer Resource Center, one in four college students has an STD. And, statistics...[show] that although people ages fifteen to twenty-four represent only 25 percent of the sexually active population, they account for more than half of the new STD diagnoses each year."
>
> —Laura Berman, PhD[2]

What Is the Difference Between STDs and STIs?

STD stands for sexually transmitted disease and STI stands for sexually transmitted infection. Essentially, the difference between the two is that an STD is an STI that has been in the body, untreated, for long enough that it has progressed from an infection to a disease. When detected and treated early, many STIs can be eradicated entirely and never become diseases. The use of "STI" is also meant to help avoid the social stigma surrounding "STDs."

Here are a few facts:

- By age twenty-five, one in two sexually active people will have contracted an STI.[3]
- STIs are among the most common infections in the U.S. today.
- Twenty million new infections occur every year.[4]
- Most STIs can be easily cured or treated if they are caught early.
- Left untreated, some STIs can lead to more serious health problems, such as cervical cancer or infertility; some can even be fatal.
- You do not need to have intercourse to contract an STI. They can be spread through any exchange of bodily fluids (including of blood and saliva), or by simple skin-to-skin contact.

For more information, visit plannedparenthood.org, beforeplay.org/stds/ uncovering-stds, or cdc.gov/reproductivehealth/unintendedpregnancy/ contraception.htm. The book *Seductive Delusions: How Everyday People Catch STDs*, by Jill Grimes, is also a worthwhile read.

Cindy's Take

Health educators provide extensive education about STIs to students of all ages, yet many students just can't help themselves from taking the risk. One young woman explains, "I know better, but I assume… or hope people I hook up with have been tested. Being treated at the clinic for an STI was so embarrassing. When I hook up with someone, it seems too awkward to have a whole conversation about whether or not they have been tested, so I usually hope for the best. You would think I would not make the same mistake again, but it took two rounds of the same STI for me to get it. I try to warn my friends, but they don't listen."

Common STIs

In the following section, I answer questions about STI symptoms, treatment, and testing, starting with the most common STIs.

HPV (Human Papillomavirus) and Genital Warts

Type: Viral

How common is it? Extremely. HPV is the most common STI; at least 50 percent of sexually active people will get it at some point.

What are the symptoms? There are many different strains of HPV, some of which are more serious than others. HPV will often go away on its own. The strains that do not, however, can cause genital warts or cervical cancer.

How do I get tested? Because there are so many strains of HPV, there is no single general test. For women, a gynecologist can perform an HPV test at the same time that you get a Pap smear; the Pap test itself checks for abnormal cervical cells, which would be a symptom of an HPV infection, though not for HPV itself. There is no routine test that has yet been developed for men. For both genders, genital warts are diagnosed through a visual examination performed by a doctor.

What is treatment like? HPV itself does not require treatment, only its symptoms do. This is because HPV is a virus and therefore not completely curable. It is, however, very manageable.

Treatment for cervical cancer is a complicated and extensive process that your doctor will discuss with you, should you be diagnosed.

Treatment for genital warts includes the following options:

- Doctor-prescribed creams and medications
- Removal by freezing with liquid nitrogen
- Removal by treatment with trichloroacetic or bichloroacetic acid
- Application of a tincture of ointment by a doctor
- Removal by scalpel, scissors, curette, or electro-surgery

How can I avoid contracting it? Gardasil is a vaccine for HPV, which is usually administered when boys and girls are eleven to twelve years old. The goal is for young people to be vaccinated before they have sexual contact with a partner who may already be infected. If you haven't been vaccinated yet, it's not too late! You can still get the vaccine through age twenty-six (both men and women). Gardasil works to prevent the strains of HPV that most commonly cause cervical cancers and warts. It is delivered as a series of three injections over the course of six months.

Condoms and dental dams will help but are not a guaranteed method for preventing the transmission of the infection, because HPV spreads through skin-to-skin contact rather than the exchange of bodily fluids.

Herpes

Type: Viral

There are two strands of this virus, called HSV-1 (herpes simplex virus type 1) and HSV-2 (herpes simplex virus type 2). Although both strains can cause blisters on both the mouth and the genital area, in general HSV-1 is associated with oral herpes and HSV-2 with genital herpes. New estimates, however, emphasize the fact that HSV-1 is also a frequent cause of genital herpes.[5] Once people become sexually active, there is a high risk of contracting HSV-1 genitally through oral sex. Approximately 140 million people aged fifteen to forty-nine are infected with genital HSV-1 infection, primarily in Western nations.[6] Both HSV-1 and HSV-2 are highly contagious, and there is no cure for herpes.

According to WHO's first global estimates, "More than 3.7 billion people under the age of 50—or 67% of the population—are infected with herpes simplex virus type 1 (HSV-1).[7]

How common is it? The CDC estimates that one in every six people aged fourteen to forty-nine years has genital herpes.[8] Jill Grimes of Johns Hopkins Medicine estimates that 50 to 90 percent of adults in the U.S. have oral herpes by age fifty.[9] According to Grimes, 90 percent of the 25 percent of adults who have HSV-2 don't know they have it.[10] In recent years, there has been a significant increase in the percentage of cases of genital herpes caused by HSV-1 because of oral-genital sex.[11]

If I have cold sores, does that mean I have genital herpes? Cold sores do not indicate that you have genital herpes. Although the same virus can cause outbreaks in both locations, there must be skin-to-skin contact in order for it to spread to new parts of the body. This means that there is some risk in, for instance, touching your mouth while you have a cold sore outbreak and then touching your genital area; you could spread the virus to yourself. It will never spontaneously appear on your genitals just because you have the virus in your bloodstream, however.

What are the symptoms? Herpes lesions are described as cold sores on the mouth or genitals. Herpes appears as one or a cluster of small blisters with a bright red base. Often, people feel a burning, itching, or tingling sensation in the affected area prior to the appearance of lesions.

It is worth noting that these symptoms are in no way life-threatening (unless you have a severely weakened immune system as a result of another condition). Though herpes is highly stigmatized, it is actually one of the least harmful and most common STIs. It is precisely that stigma that causes herpes to be spread; people fear telling partners of their infection because they do not want to be rejected or thought of as contaminated, and the couple therefore does not take the necessary precautions to avoid transmission.

How can I get tested? Blood tests can screen for the presence of HSV antibodies. The presence of these antibodies, however, does not tell us as much as we might like. It does not allow us to distinguish between HSV-1 and HSV-2, nor does it tell us what parts of the body are actually affected by lesions.

What is treatment like? There is no cure for either strain of HSV. You can work to prevent outbreaks by avoiding triggers (triggers generally include stress, illness, sunlight, certain foods, and, for women, their periods). The amino acid lysine has been shown to help with cold sores. Lysine can be ingested from some foods or in pill supplement form, and can be applied topically as a cream.

For oral herpes, a variety of creams exist to treat lesions when they occur. Some over-the-counter options are: Abreva, Herpecin-L, Orajel, and creams containing lysine. Prescription-strength antiretrovirals also exist as creams and in pill form. There are pills that can be taken daily to prevent the frequency of outbreaks.

How can I avoid contracting it? HSV is extremely contagious and is spread through skin-to-skin contact. Though it is spread most easily when an infected person has an active outbreak, it can be spread even when there are no visible symptoms. Use condoms for vaginal or anal intercourse *and* during oral sex. If you do have a lesion, doctors generally say that you are most contagious from the first "tingle" until after the lesion has visibly cleared. You can, however, always be contagious even when you don't have symptoms.

Chlamydia

Type: Bacterial (the *Chlamydia trachomatis* bacteria)

How common is it? Planned Parenthood lists chlamydia as "the most common sexually transmitted bacterial infection in the United States," stating that around three million Americans are infected each year (which makes chlamydia three times more common than gonorrhea and fifty times more common than syphilis).[12]

What are the symptoms? Chlamydia usually has no symptoms. When it does, they include genital pain and unusual discharge. Women sometimes also have pain in the abdomen or lower back, nausea, spotting, or pain during sex.

It is worth noting that chlamydia can also be spread to the anus, mouth, or throat through anal and oral sex.

How do I get tested? A urine test will check for chlamydia. For women, a cervical or vaginal swab is also an option.

What is treatment like? Chlamydia is easily treated with antibiotics, either a one-day or seven-day course. Usual rules for antibiotics apply: don't share, take them all, and wait until the treatment is done before you have sex again. Reinfection is common, and having chlamydia more than once puts you at a higher risk for long-term consequences.

How can I avoid contracting it? Use latex condoms whenever you have vaginal, anal, or oral sex.

Gonorrhea ("The clap")

Type: Bacterial (the *Neisseria gonorrhoeae* bacteria)

How common is it? Gonorrhea is very common, particularly among younger people. The CDC estimates 820,000 new gonorrheal infections occur annually in the U.S., 570,000 of them in fifteen- to twenty-five-year-olds.[13]

What are the symptoms? Both men and women are often asymptomatic (especially women). When men do have symptoms, they can include yellow, white, or green discharge from the penis; burning upon urination; and swollen or painful testicles. In women, symptoms can easily be confused with other infections, as they typically include abnormal vaginal discharge or spotting. If left untreated, gonorrhea can cause pelvic inflammatory disease (PID) in women, the symptoms and complications of which are outlined later in this chapter. Because symptoms are so difficult to detect, it is important to be screened regularly for gonorrhea. Left untreated, the infection can cause sterility in both men and women.

How do I get tested? A urine test can check for gonorrhea.

What is treatment like? Gonorrhea is curable and must be treated with a round of antibiotics. As with all antibiotics, it is important that you finish the round of treatment, even if symptoms have gone away. Do not give your medication to anyone else. Wait a week after finishing the antibiotics before having sex again.

How can I avoid contracting it? Use latex condoms whenever you have vaginal, anal, or oral sex.

Syphilis

Type: Bacterial (the *Treponema pallidum* bacteria)

How common is it? Syphilis is one of the less common STIs for the majority of the population. It is primarily seen among men who have sex with men, though it does, of course, also occur within other populations.

What are the symptoms? Syphilis is tricky because if you don't catch the first symptoms, they will go away and the bacteria will remain dormant in your body for years, potentially causing serious long-term effects. In what is called the "primary stage" of a syphilis infection, a sore (called a "chancre") will appear on the genitals, mouth, or anus of the person infected. This sore is generally painless, small, and firm. There is often only one sore, but there can be multiple.

While that sore is healing or a few weeks after it is gone, untreated syphilis will progress into the "secondary stage." The most notable aspect of secondary-stage syphilis is a non-itchy body rash that can show up on the palms of your hands and soles of your feet, all over your body, or in just a few places. You could also be infected with syphilis and have very mild symptoms or none at all.

What are the serious long-term effects? If syphilis is not detected and treated during the primary or secondary stages, it will go into a "latent stage" in which there are no symptoms. This can last years, during which the bacteria remain in the body undetected. In some people, syphilis will then develop into the "late stage," ten to thirty years after initial infection. Symptoms of late-stage syphilis include serious neurological conditions such as loss of muscular control (sometimes to the point of paralysis), blindness, and dementia. Seriously bad news.

How do I get tested? A health provider can perform a blood test to check for syphilis; in some cases, a sample of the fluid from a sore can also confirm diagnosis.

What is treatment like? Antibiotics are prescribed to treat syphilis. However, if syphilis has reached a late stage it may have already done damage to the body that the antibiotics cannot heal.

How can I avoid contracting it? Use latex condoms whenever you have vaginal, anal, or oral sex.

Pubic Lice ("Crabs")

Type: Parasitic

How common is it? The American Sexual Health Association reports that there are "an estimated 3 million cases of crabs every year" in the U.S. [14]

Can I get it from someone even if we don't have sex? You can contract pubic lice from another person through close physical contact, even if that contact does not include sex. Pubic lice can also be spread through infected bedding, clothing, furniture, or toilet seats, but this is much less common.

What are the symptoms? Pubic lice cause intense itching in the infected area. That is because the lice feed on blood and are constantly biting you. Often, there will also be small blue dots at the bite sites. You can usually see the lice as well. Pubic lice are most famously found in pubic hair, but can also live in hair on other parts of the body, including the eyebrows, eyelashes, face, armpits, legs, and so on.

How do I get tested? Most people can self diagnose by examining the area either with the naked eye or with a magnifying glass. Adult pubic lice look like small, gray crabs (hence the nickname) that become engorged and darken in color after feeding on blood. The nits, or eggs, are also usually visible: they look like small, yellowish white ovals attached to the shafts of hairs.

What is treatment like? There are a number of pills, lotions, and gels that can be used to treat pubic lice. Some of these are over-the-counter treatments; if those options don't work for you, however, you can get stronger options with a prescription from your doctor.

If you have pubic lice, you may also want to thoroughly clean all fabrics that you have come into contact with by machine-washing in hot water. Any items that are not machine washable can be dry-cleaned or stored for two weeks in a sealed plastic bag.

How can I avoid contracting it? No barrier method will protect against pubic lice, including condoms. The only way to avoid getting them is to avoid close physical contact with an infected person altogether. Given that the lice are spread so easily during physical contact, it is important that you tell any recent sexual partners that you have discovered pubic lice on yourself so that they may seek treatment before their infection gets worse.

Hepatitis

Type: Viral

There are a bunch of different kinds of hepatitis, right? There are five strains of hepatitis, differentiated as hepatitis A, B, C, D, and E. Doctors in the United States are most concerned about strains A, B, and C; hepatitis B is the strain most commonly transmitted through sexual activity. As a blanket term, "hepatitis" simply means an infection of the liver (the prefix "hepa-" means liver). I'll walk through A, B, and C below.

Hepatitis A: Hepatitis A (HAV) is most often transmitted through fecal contact (most commonly, fecal–oral contact). This means that, in a sexual context, anal sex bears a high risk of transmitting the virus.

Although HAV is the only strain that usually does not cause chronic problems for the infected individual, it is still extremely important to identify it early on. HAV is often asymptomatic, but if it does cause symptoms they include those most common to liver failure, such as jaundice, abdominal pain, dark urine, fever, and fatigue. Most people recover completely and do not have any lasting liver damage, although they may feel sick for months. The rare cases in which hepatitis A causes total liver failure and death most commonly occur in persons fifty years of age or older and persons with other liver diseases, such as hepatitis B or C.

Hepatitis B: This is the hepatitis strain that sexual health experts are most concerned with, because hepatitis B (HBV) is the only strain of hepatitis that is transmitted through bodily fluids like semen and saliva. It is also transmitted through infective blood, meaning that shared needles or other exposure to another's blood can put you at risk for contracting the virus.

The most serious problems with HBV are not the symptoms experienced immediately after infection (during the acute phase) but rather those that can come later, if the body is unable to fight the virus and it causes chronic liver damage (more on that later). In the acute phase, hepatitis B can manifest as fever, fatigue, and the usual signs of liver damage (as noted above, these can include jaundice, abdominal pain, dark urine, clay-colored bowel movements, and vomiting). During the chronic phase, as liver damage worsens, these same symptoms intensify and can become fatal.

Hepatitis C: HCV is most often transmitted through exposure to contaminated blood. This exposure can occur when individuals share needles, or when people fail to use adequate barriers when dealing with another's blood during medical care or otherwise.

HCV is asymptomatic in most people, during both the acute and chronic phases. Hepatitis C is a slow, progressive disease, lasting ten to forty years until liver damage becomes serious enough to have major health impacts.

What are the long-term effects of hepatitis? Although a small group of individuals with hepatitis will develop acute liver failure and die, for the majority of cases the real danger lies in the long-term effects. HAV can, luckily, be resolved by the body in most cases and will not progress past the acute phase. HBV and HCV, however, can cause chronic liver problems. This only occurs in 10 percent of cases,[15] but when it does occur it can lead to liver cancer or cirrhosis. Those at greatest risk for developing chronic infections are children under six years of age; the majority of college-age students can fight off the infection.

How do I get tested? Blood tests check for antibodies to hepatitis A, B, and C. Even with a blood test, it is difficult to distinguish between the various strains.

What is treatment like? There is no cure for HAV, HBV, or HCV. Getting vaccinated is a good idea, and if you are not vaccinated but get exposed, there are courses of post-exposure prophylaxis available to stop the virus from multiplying. It is a lifelong disease, however, and in the (relatively rare) cases where the infected individual does not clear the disease on his own, treatment is largely aimed at improving comfort and quality of life.

How can I avoid contracting it? The good news about hepatitis is that vaccines are available for hepatitis A, B, D, and E. Most schools require that enrolled students have at least the HBV vaccine, and thanks to this practice, rates of hepatitis infection are dropping in the United States. As such, hepatitis is not a common STD here; it's more of a problem in developing countries where there is less access to the vaccines.

If you are not vaccinated (you can find out by asking your doctor to check your vaccination records), you can avoid contracting hepatitis by:

- HAV—avoiding contact with fecal matter or potentially contaminated food and water
- HBV—using condoms and avoiding sexual contact with infected individuals
- HCV—avoiding exposure to infective blood. Remember, there is no vaccine for HCV so there is greater danger in exposure.

Pelvic Inflammatory Disease (PID)

Type: Bacterial

What exactly is PID? PID is an infection of the female reproductive organs. PID is not caused by a single type of bacteria; rather, it is a complication that results from other infections. PID most commonly occurs when a woman has an infection—particularly an STI like chlamydia or gonorrhea—and the bacteria travel from her vagina into other parts of her reproductive organs such as the cervix, uterus, and fallopian tubes. PID is not caused only by STIs, however; many different bacteria can cause infections in these organs. PID may have serious consequences for your reproductive and overall health, with potential complications including long-term pelvic pain and an increased risk of ectopic pregnancy.

Can only women get PID? Only women get PID; however, if a woman has PID, another infection is likely present in her body, which could be transmitted to her partner.

What are the symptoms? PID can often be asymptomatic. When symptoms do occur (generally during the first five to ten days of the menstrual cycle), they manifest as:

- Pain or tenderness in the lower abdomen, cervix, or uterus, during sex or otherwise
- Unusual, bad-smelling discharge
- Fever or chills
- A burning sensation during urination
- Bleeding between periods

How do I get tested? It is important to see a doctor if you think you have PID; infections in the reproductive organs can be difficult to diagnose on your own and infections in the reproductive organs pose a serious danger to your future fertility; this danger increases the longer the infection is left untreated. Before diagnosing PID, doctors will usually attempt to rule out other STIs.

What is treatment like? Treatment for PID is usually a round of antibiotics, prescribed by a doctor. Take all of the pills you are prescribed, and wait to have sex until after you have finished the antibiotics. In more serious cases, PID may require antibiotics to be delivered through an IV or it may necessitate hospitalization—all the more reason to see your doctor early if you have any suspicious symptoms.

How can I avoid contracting it? Condoms protect against many of the types of bacteria that cause PID.

HIV/AIDS (Human Immunodeficiency Virus/Acquired Immunodeficiency Syndrome)

Type: Viral

Why are there two acronyms? What's the difference? HIV is a virus that, over time, causes AIDS. AIDS itself is not a transmissible disease: it is the last and most serious stage of HIV infection, not its own virus.

How does the virus work? HIV attacks a person's immune system (specifically, the T-cells), making the body less and less capable of fighting off infections. This immune-compromised state, once it reaches a certain degree of severity, is AIDS.

HIV is transmitted through bodily fluids. This means that unprotected sex with an infected partner and exposure to contaminated blood (by sharing needles or other means) are the primary modes of HIV transmission.

What are the symptoms? It's hard to pin down specific symptoms as being indicative of HIV. The disease's most serious consequence is that it makes a person susceptible to *other* illnesses, so symptoms may range widely, depending on the person's exposures.

HIV progresses in stages, and it is during the first, or acute, stage that notable symptoms may appear. These are generally flu-like symptoms, which may be difficult to differentiate from normal illness. Some people may not have symptoms at all during the acute phase, which usually lasts two to four weeks.

The second stage is called "clinical latency," and is essentially a period during which HIV is reproducing at lower levels, so the individual will not notice many effects of the infection. It is at this stage that most HIV-infected individuals live for years.

The final stage of an HIV infection is the development of AIDS, which is defined by a CD4 cell (also known as T-helper cells) count below two hundred cells/mm.[16] At this point, the immune system becomes so damaged that patients are extremely vulnerable to outside infections, and so will often become quite sick; though again, the specific symptoms are dependent on which outside infections they are exposed to.

I have heard that only gay men get HIV. Is this true? It is absolutely not true that HIV infects only gay men. HIV can, and does, affect people of all sexual orientations, gender identities, and races. According to CDC statistics, 25 percent of new HIV infections in 2010 in the U.S. occurred through heterosexual sex.[17]

How do I get tested? A doctor will usually test for HIV with a "rapid test" that takes fifteen to twenty minutes and requires either a sample of your blood or a swab of the inside of your cheek. Depending on the results of that test and/or how you score on other risk factors, a doctor may also perform a more intensive blood test that must be processed by a lab, which will take about a week. It is also important to note that HIV is often not detected in the blood for three weeks to six months after it is contracted.

What is treatment like? There is no cure for HIV, so a positive diagnosis means a lifelong process of disease management. Antiretroviral drugs (which limit the reproduction of viruses in the body) have shown some effectiveness in the treatment of HIV. These are coupled with general lifestyle choices to improve overall health and limit exposure to infection. Truvada is a prescription medicine used to treat HIV-1 infection and is always used together with other HIV-1 medicines.[18] Truvada also helps reduce the risk of becoming infected with HIV-1 infection when used with safer sex practices.[19]

Until recent years, a positive HIV diagnosis was basically considered a death sentence. Thanks to progress in medical treatments and in public awareness, however, it is becoming increasingly likely that people can essentially halt the progression of AIDS development for decades at a time and continue to live full and productive lives with HIV.

How can I avoid contracting it? Condom use during sexual activity is the most effective means of preventing transmission of HIV.

Also avoid exposing yourself to the blood of others by using barriers like latex gloves if administering medical treatment, and never share needles. Truvada can help reduce the risk of contracting HIV.

Talking About Birth Control

Discussing contraception with a sexual partner can be awkward, but it is absolutely necessary. Once again, if that conversation feels too unbearable, that may be an indicator that your choice to have sex with that person might not be a healthy one at that time. Feelings of awkwardness can be a signal to pay attention to what is motivating your choice to engage in sexual activity with that person. If you choose to avoid a conversation about contraception, you should be prepared to have an even more difficult conversation about what it would be like for you both to be parents at this point in your lives, to give a baby up for adoption, or to terminate a pregnancy. Fifty-one percent of pregnancies are unintended.[20] The risk of becoming pregnant in college inspires many sexually active college women to use a method of highly effective reversible contraception (HERC), and the risk of contracting an STI doesn't always inspire follow-through to use condoms. Condoms should be used in conjunction with another device and should not be relied on as the primary method of contraception.

Contraceptive Methods

The following information about contraceptive methods is from the *Effectiveness of Family Planning Methods* by the Centers for Disease

Control and Prevention (CDC).[21] The percentages given indicate the number out of every one hundred women who experienced an unintended pregnancy within the first year of typical use of each contraceptive method.

Most Effective Birth Control Methods (less than 1 pregnancy per 100 women in a year)

Reversible options (highly effective reversible contraception—HERC):
Implant .05%
Intrauterine Device (IUD) .2% (a small amount of synthetic hormone is released each day and acts locally in the uterus to prevent pregnancy, instead of going throughout your whole body, the way the pill or some other hormonal methods do.
Copper IUD .8% (no hormones)
   Once in place, there is little or nothing to do or remember.

Permanent sterilization:
Female (Abdominal, Lapraroscopic, and Hysteroscopic) .5%
Male (Vasectomy) .15%
   After the procedure, there is little or nothing to do or remember. Use another contraceptive method for the first three months.

Effective Birth Control Methods (6–12 pregnancies per 100 women in a year)

Injectable 6% Get a shot every 3 months.
Pill 9% Take pill each day on time.
Patch 9% Keep in place, change on time.
Ring 9% Keep in place, change on time.
Diaphragm 12% Use correctly every time you have sex.

Least Effective Birth Control Methods (18 or more pregnancies per 100 women in a year)

Male condom 18%
Female condom 21%
NOTE: Condoms should always be used along with other methods to reduce the risk of sexually transmitted infections, whether or not they are your primary method of birth control.
Withdrawal 22%
Sponge
   Nulliparous women (women who have not borne children) 12%
   Parous women (women who have borne children) 24%
Fertility awareness–based methods 24%
Spermacide 28%

The Morning After

The morning-after pill and IUD insertion after unprotected sex are last-resort efforts to prevent pregnancy after another method of birth control has failed. Morning-after pills can be purchased in most pharmacies for $30 to $50, depending on the brand. There is no age requirement to buy the morning-after pill.

Make Sure You Talk About It!

Before you engage in sexual activity with a partner, you should both be tested for STIs, get educated about birth control options, communicate with each other about the options, and make sure you are prepared to use the birth control method and protection properly. Taking all of these steps is your best chance to avoid pregnancy and protect yourself from contracting or spreading STIs.

College students report that communicating about sex, contraception, and safer sex is challenging. Sometimes it just takes one of you to initiate a conversation, and the rest of the discussion and preparation go smoothly. It is common, though, for people to go along with whatever is happening and skip birth control "just this one time" because it seems easier. Sometimes people allow their intoxication, arousal, or both to get in the way of starting the conversation. There is no good reason *not* to have this talk. Get serious about practicing communication around sex so you can stay safe and healthy. It really does get easier with practice. Having a plan in place—a script of what you will say—makes it easier to assert your standards and expectations with a sexual partner.

Conviction helps set the tone of the conversation, and if being assertive scares a partner off, be grateful you weeded out someone who would put having sex ahead of your physical and emotional health and well-being. Muster up the courage and make these conversations happen.

A Final Word

The purpose of college is social, emotional, and cognitive growth—it's an incredible opportunity to enrich your mind, to spark some passion deep within you, to learn in a supportive and intellectual environment, and to identify strengths that will help you find your way in the world. What you choose for a major may or may not be related to what you end up doing for a job, but it will get you on a path and expose you to a variety of information and perspectives that will expand your worldview. In short, college is about being open to experience.

In the words of my wise and close college friend, "College is the only time you will be a five-minute walk from twenty-five of your closest friends." Often, the most significant, yet nebulous, aspect of the college experience is the social scene; it can play a major role in the experience for most people. The volume and velocity of social interactions consume a lot of psychic space when you live in close proximity with a lot of people. A major part of many students' college experience is gathering with people in the dorm, in the dining hall, on the lawn, along the walkways, at the student center, at events, or at parties. Regardless of where people stand on the spectrum of interest in sexual relationships, the topic of sex commands a lot of conversation and attention among students. Whether you have been sexually active with partners for years or sexual relationships aren't even on your radar at this point, you will be navigating some version of the hookup culture on your college campus, for sure.

Taking into account current research, reports from recent graduates and current students, and strong messages from campus health centers, here is the bottom line:

1. Avoid going along mindlessly with expectations and accepted norms that are created and perpetuated on social media. Follow your own inner compass to find what feels right for you.
2. It is possible to be safe and have fun in the new world of sexual communication if you choose your sexual partners carefully and consciously and communicate openly and directly.
3. Prepare yourself with accurate information about all the influences on your social and sexual choices.
4. Join or start the conversation on your campus about consent, sexual assault, the influence of porn, the role of alcohol and drugs, sexual orientation, gender identity, contraception, and STIs to help you and your peers make healthy social and sexual decisions.

Informed choices help people find friendships and relationships that make them feel good and lead to authentic intimacy and connection. It is imperative that you enter college armed with the facts and a clear understanding of what you will most likely encounter socially and sexually. If you do so, surely you will increase your chances of having a positive, socially meaningful time. What could be better than that?

Resources

Resources for Sexual Assault Survivors

Check out your campus resources. These will, of course, vary from campus to campus in how helpful and comprehensive they are. Most campuses are expanding prevention programs, improving support for survivors, and adding resources. *Note*: be sure to identify ahead of time which campus resources are confidential, and which will automatically file reports with the administration.

The National Sexual Assault Hotline—800-656-HOPE (4673)—is a free, safe, and confidential service run by RAINN that gives you 24–7 access to:

- Confidential, judgment-free support from a trained staff member
- Support finding a local health facility that is trained to care for survivors of sexual assault and offers services like sexual assault forensic exams
- Someone to help you talk through what happened
- Local resources that can assist with your next steps toward healing and recovery

- Referrals for long-term support in your area
- Information about the laws in your area
- Basic information about medical concerns[1]

RAINN is the Rape, Abuse & Incest National Network. Find out more at www.rainn.org.

End Rape on Campus (EROC) works to end campus sexual violence through direct support for survivors and their communities; prevention through education; and policy reform at the campus, local, state, and federal levels. Find out more at endrapeoncampus.org.

Loveisrespect specializes in dating violence and provides free and confidential support from highly trained peer advocates. Call 1-866-331-9474, text "loveis" to 22522 to anonymously text a trained supporter, or chat online at loveisrespect.org.

FORGE serves transgender and gender-nonconforming survivors of domestic and sexual violence and provides referrals to local counselors. http://forge-forward.org/

The Anti-Violence Project serves people who are LGBTQ; hotline 212-714-1124; nilingual 24–7. http://www.avp.org/

National Sexual Violence Resource Center provides resources and information relating to all aspects of sexual violence; toll-free hotline 1-877-739-3895. http://www.nsvrc.org/

National Domestic Violence Hotline: 1-800-799-7233. A 24–7 confidential hotline dedicated to providing resources and support for victims of domestic abuse. http://www.thehotline.org/

Sexual Assault Vocabulary to Know

Acquaintance rape (also called date rape): An instance of rape in which the perpetrator and the victim had a previous relationship. This can include but is not limited to: classmates, friends, casual acquaintances, and current or ex-significant others. This category makes up the vast majority of rape cases, and is further subdivided into date rape and general acquaintance rape.

The Campus Sexual Violence Elimination (SaVE) Act refers to the Violence Against Women Act (VAWA) amendment to the Clery Act. The Campus SaVE Act expands the scope of this legislation in terms of reporting, response, and prevention education requirements[2] and imposes new reporting requirements to include domestic violence, dating violence, and stalking.

The Clery Act: Originally passed in 1990 and since expanded, the Clery Act mandates that schools release public annual reports of the crimes committed on their campuses. This includes both forcible and nonforcible sex offenses. The website for End Rape on Campus (EROC) describes the Clery Act as follows:

> The Jeanne Clery Disclosure of Campus Security Policy and Campus Crime Statistics Act (known as the Clery Act) is a federal law requiring United States colleges and universities to disclose information about crime on and around their campuses. The Act is enforced by the United States Department of Education. The Clery Act requires colleges and universities to do the following with regards to sexual assault reports: 1) Publish an Annual Security Report; 2) Disclose crime statistics for incidents that occur on campus,

in unobstructed public areas immediately adjacent to or running through the campus and at certain non-campus facilities; 3) Issue timely warnings about Clery Act crimes which pose a serious or ongoing threat to students and employees; and 4) Devise an emergency response, notification, and testing policy.[3]

Dating violence: Dating violence is a pattern of assaultive (physical and sexual) and controlling behaviors that one person uses against another in order to gain or maintain power and control in the relationship. The abuser intentionally behaves in ways that cause fear, degradation, intimidation, coercion, isolation, and humiliation to control the other person. Forms of abuse can be physical, sexual, emotional, and/or psychological. Victims and abusers come from all social and economic backgrounds, faith communities, and racial and ethnic backgrounds. Abuse also occurs in same-sex relationships. Both females and males can be victims of dating violence, but numerous studies reveal the reality that the majority of victims are female (usually more than 95 percent).[4]

Perpetrator: Also often referred to as the "assailant" or "attacker" in a sexual assault, "perpetrator" refers to an individual who has committed a crime.

Rape: "Unwanted sexual penetration (vaginal, anal, oral, or object penetration by an offender) achieved either through physical force, threat of force, or incapacitation of the victim,"[5] as defined by the Campus Sexual Assault Study, performed by the National Institute of Justice from 2005 to 2007.

Rape kit or Sexual Assault Examination Kit (SAEK): A forensic exam that a survivor can choose to have performed after their assault. This exam takes place at a hospital and is performed by either a SANE or a SAFE (see below). Not all hospitals have individuals who have been trained as either SANEs or SAFEs; to locate one near you that does have examiners, call the National Sexual Assault Hotline at 800-656-4673.

The exam is most effective if the survivor has not yet showered, gone to the bathroom, or eaten, but if you have done these things, do not be deterred from seeking an examination, as there still may be evidence. This is a legal procedure rather than a medical procedure.

This thorough examination occurs in two parts: first, the nurse will ask for a verbal account of the assault, with as much detail as possible. The survivor can, of course, choose how much information she or he wishes to disclose, but a more complete narrative contributes to a more comprehensive examination. Second, the SANE will physically examine the survivor. This examination will be somewhat invasive, but is done to obtain as much information as possible in the hope of treating the physical effects of the assault and potentially identifying the perpetrator. The physical section of the SANE examination typically consists of a swab of the pelvic area; a speculum exam (if the assault involved intercourse); swabs of any other parts of the body that the survivor indicates; nail clippings; hair samples; photographs; and blood and urine samples. The examiner will also offer to test for some common STIs/STDs—including HIV/AIDS—and pregnancy.

SANE (Sexual Assault Nurse Examiner): A registered nurse who has completed specialized education and clinical preparation in the medical forensic care of the patient who has experienced sexual assault or abuse, as defined by the International Association of Forensic Nurses.[6] If a survivor goes to the hospital within 120 hours after an assault, a SANE will perform an examination. **SAFE** (Sexual Assault Forensic Examiners) refers to other healthcare professionals who have been instructed and trained to complete the exam by providing evaluation, treatment referral, and follow-up.[7]

Sexual assault: Any type of sexual contact or behavior that occurs without the explicit consent of the recipient. Falling under the definition of sexual assault are sexual activities such as forced sexual intercourse, forcible sodomy, child molestation, incest, fondling, and attempted rape.[8]

Statutory rape: Sexual acts between a legal adult and a legal minor. These acts are illegal, even when the sexual acts are consensual. Statutory rape laws vary from state to state, particularly with regard to the age of consent. In some states, it is the age differential that matters.[9]

Stranger rape: An instance of rape in which the perpetrator and the victim had no prior relationship.

Survivor: In the context of this book, a person who has experienced a sexual assault. The term *survivor* is often used instead of *victim* because survivor has fewer negative implications and does not carry the assumption that the individual feels "victimized."

Title IX: A federal civil rights law passed in the Education Amendments of 1972 that prohibits discrimination on the basis of sex in any federally funded education program or activity.[10] Because "sex discrimination" includes sexual harassment and assault, Title IX establishes the legal standards on which schools must base their sexual violence policies. Most of the current lawsuits filed by students against their colleges (Amherst, Yale, Columbia) are based on the charge that the way those institutions handled cases of sexual assault on campus failed to adequately uphold Title IX standards.

Program Models for Sexual Assault Prevention Efforts

The Date Safe Project

Mike Domitrz, founder of the Date Safe Project (datesafeproject. org), has become one of the most sought-after experts that communities, the military, the media, and universities turn to for programs that address consent, bystander intervention, and support for survivors. Mike brings his unique combination of humor, storytelling, role-playing, skills teaching, vulnerability, and inclusiveness to his programs, trainings, live events, and educational products.

Here is Mike's perspective on campuses addressing sexual assault:

Is your goal to reduce the number of sexual assaults happening within your campus community? Is your goal to help create a culture of respect and consent? If you are a student or a leader in an educational institution or a community, your goal should be *both*— reduce sexual violence while building a culture of respect and consent. Unfortunately, too many schools are so focused on short-term goals such as meeting federal requirements that they are missing the long-term objective that would have the greatest impact on reducing sexual violence now and in the future: **cultural transformation** (if the program is done well, the outcome will be in compliance with federal requirements).

The key to cultural transformation is giving students realistic skill sets, the confidence, and the "why" to create a culture built on respect and consent. You need all three components. Too many schools are focused on raising awareness. The problem with focusing on awareness is that the majority of students already know the right answers to give, even as they exhibit behaviors contrary to those answers.

Ask students, "Can a person who is not of sound mind give consent?" and almost every student knows the answer is no. However, some of those same students will intentionally pursue drunken sexual intimacy later that weekend.

Student pass an online or printed training quiz, then walk away thinking, "That was stupid. No one is actually going to actually do that."

The worst part of this approach is the harm being done. Bad training means that, when students remember the last time they participated in training, they recall that it was boring and/or ineffective (whether standardized online training or in person). The outcome is students who don't want to attend future trainings. Bad training also leads students to think, "That was so stupid—it just proves this whole 'sexual assault' thing is overblown." Educational efforts to reduce sexual violence that lead *people to believe that sexual assault is not a problem are not acceptable.*

Training focused on creating a culture of respect and consent needs to be fantastic in both the approach and the strategies utilized throughout. We need to raise the bar of expectations for what is most likely to work in transforming the campus culture into one based on consent and respect. The three essential components needed for a student to make positive behavior changes in building a culture of consent and respect are realistic skill sets, confidence, and "why" (a reason).

Without **realistic skill sets**, people will rationalize their own behavior, thinking, "Yes, the current system is messed up, but what can I do about it?" or "Asking first sounds good, but in reality it just doesn't work." These are excuses made by people who have never been given a **realistic skill set** and shown how to "ask first" in a way they are confident implementing in their own lives.

Confidence matters. The less confidence people have, the less likely they will engage in their own lives and in the lives of others.

I work with the military throughout the world. Their daily responsibilities can involve life-and-death situations. How do they make quick decisions? Confidence in knowing what they are doing is right. How do they get that confidence? Practice.

Some people will rehearse in their mind or with friends (role-playing). A great example would be talking through this with your healthy crew. Discuss different scenarios. If someone says, "Yeah, but that won't work," follow up with, "How *can* we make it work?"

Rehearsing is great for all forms of talking and bystander intervention. You gain confidence, which greatly increases the likelihood you will engage in the right choices to make a positive impact going forward.

The "**why**" is the biggest aspect many educational efforts fail to include in trainings. Why do *you* deserve to always have a choice? Why does every person always deserve to have a choice? Why is the potential victim of a predator at a bar or party worthy of your intervention? Why are you going to be willing to have a difficult conversation with loved ones, letting them know that they can come to you if they ever are (or have ever been) sexually assaulted?

Your "**why**" is the number-one factor you need in order to intervene in your own life and/or in the lives of others, including strangers.

Speak About It

Speak About It is a program that seeks to promote bystander intervention and improve students' understanding of consent.

Executive Director Shana Natelson and Program Director Kaylee Wolfe summarize the mission of Speak About It:

Most people don't think that teaching healthy sexual boundaries and communication is a form of sexual assault prevention, but that's exactly what Speak About It does with high school and college students. Through an entertaining, educational, and empowering hour-long performance, Speak About It challenges students' perception of consent, illustrates realities about sexual assault, and encourages bystander intervention with peers. Using a careful mix of thoughtful humor and honest storytelling, the performance works to shift the conversation about sexual assault prevention by teaching what healthy sexual relationships can and should look like. Engaging students through humor and familiarity at the beginning of the show sets the stage for the more difficult conversations about alcohol and sexual assault that happen later.

Aligned with the many states that are now creating laws around consent, Speak About It teaches the "yes means yes" model of consent by educating students about how and when to say yes. Teaching communication and confidence gives students ownership over their bodies and their sexual choices, changing the dialogue from one that focuses on stopping a behavior that is uncomfortable or unsafe to being able to ask for something that is pleasurable, safe, and desired. Think of the "yes means yes" model in terms of chocolate cake: even if we love chocolate cake, we still cut it in slices instead of diving right in. This sets boundaries and lets us adjust with each new slice. If we just start eating the whole thing, it's really hard to say no. Remember, we like cake, it tastes good, it feels good in our tummies, maybe we like the people we're eating the cake with, or maybe we're afraid if we stop eating, our friends will tell people that we don't like cake and no one will eat cake with us again (okay, maybe I'm crossing my metaphors a little here).

Let's overlay the cake metaphor with a comparison to "no means no" and "yes means yes" types of education. Eating cake is typically a pleasure-driven experience; we eat cake for no other reason than that it tastes good. Cutting a slice of cake and setting boundaries up front helps ensure that eating cake remains a pleasure-driven experience, lest we eat too much; instead of deciding up front whether or not to eat the entire cake, we can make choices as we go. And once we agree to something, we can always change our mind. Sexual activity isn't like a roller-coaster; you can change your mind and get off whenever you want.

Teaching consent using the "yes means yes" model encourages students to find their sexual boundaries by asking questions of themselves and their partners, and listening to the answers. This helps form healthy sexual boundaries and communication by empowering students to make informed decisions about their sexual choices, and this is a form of primary prevention of sexual assault.

Speak About It also teaches bystander intervention among peers. If someone looks uncomfortable or unsafe, an active bystander might ask to get a slice of pizza, suggest a bathroom break, or pretend to be friends. The role of the active bystander is not to be a superhero and drag someone away, but, similar to the way we encourage communication around consent, would ask a question and respect the answer. And each approach is different, as are we. Maybe we use humor to distract from a situation, suggest the possibility of food, or approach someone as a group if we're not comfortable on our own. We teach students that being an active bystander doesn't make you a cock block, but that if we help our friend confirm that everyone is comfortable and wants to move forward (whatever that might be), we're actually being a great wingman.

The Prevention Innovations Research Center (PIRC) at the University of New Hampshire

As a result of PIRC's innovative and transformative research, Vice President Joe Biden and Secretary of Education Arne Duncan chose UNH as the site of the announcement of the amendments to the Title IX legislation in 2011. In 2014, the PIRC was one of four research centers tapped by the White House Task Force to Protect Students from Sexual Assault to conduct extensive research. As stated on its website, the goal of the PIRC is "to end sexual and relationship violence and stalking through the power of effective researcher and practitioner partnerships."[11]

Sharyn Potter and Jane Stapleton, codirectors of PIRC, share the goals and strategies of the center's programs:

PIRC researchers and practitioners have developed two evidence-based prevention strategies, Bringing in the Bystander® In-Person Prevention Program and the Know Your Power® Bystander Social Marketing Campaign, which have been used by more than six hundred colleges and universities in the United States, Canada, and Europe, and has been adapted for the U.S. Army. Bringing in the Bystander is currently being translated into French and being adapted for high school populations. The main tenets of both programs are currently being tailored for a bystander video game for first-year college students.

Rather than focusing strictly on the roles of perpetrator and victim, the highly interactive, well researched, and evaluated Bringing in the Bystander In-Person Prevention Program uses an approach that focuses on the responsibility of the community. It teaches bystanders how to safely intervene in instances where there may be risk. The program aims to identify behaviors on a continuum of violence, develop empathy for those who have experienced violence, practice safe and appropriate intervention skills, and commit to intervening before, during, or after an incident of sexual abuse, relationship violence, or stalking occurs.

The Know Your Power Bystander Social Marketing Campaign is a nationally recognized prevention strategy focused on reducing sexual and relationship violence and stalking on college campuses. The campaign consists of a series of images that portray realistic and thought-provoking scenarios that highlight the important role all members of the community have in ending sexual assault, relationship violence, and stalking.

The images raise awareness about the problem of sexual and relationship violence and stalking, and model active bystander behaviors that audience members can use in situations where violence is occurring, has occurred, or has the potential to occur. The Know Your Power Campaign can be used on its own or in combination with the Bringing in the Bystander In-Person Prevention Program.

Over a twelve-year period, both Bringing in the Bystander and Know Your Power have been scientifically evaluated and found to be effective in improving undergraduate student attitudes, increasing knowledge, and producing positive prosocial bystander behaviors to prevent sexual and relationship violence and stalking. Participants increase their knowledge of how to safely intervene in cases of sexual and relationship violence, increase their willingness to get involved in reducing violence, and increase the likelihood that they will be active bystanders in a situation where sexual and relationship violence is about to occur, is occurring, or has occurred. The research instruments, developed and evaluated by PIRC researchers, are used by researchers and practitioners around the globe.

Glossary of Transgender and Gender-Nonconforming Terms

Adapted from *Safe & Respected* by the NYC Administration for Children's Services.[12]

Assigned sex: The sex that is noted on an individual's birth certificate issued at birth. Also referred to as sex assigned at birth or birth sex.

Biological sex: An individual's sex, male or female, based on the appearance of an individual's external genitalia and their assumed sex chromosomes.

Cisgender: A term for someone whose biological sex and gender identity are congruent. Also referred to as non-transgender.

Cross-dresser: An outdated term used to refer to someone who wears clothes of another sex/gender.

FTM/female-to-male: *See* Transgender men and boys.

Gender: The set of meanings assigned by a culture or society to someone's perceived biological sex. Gender is not static and it can shift over time. Gender has at least three components:

> **Gender identity:** Individuals' internal view of their gender; one's innermost sense of being male or female. Gender identity is well established around three to four years of age. This will often influence name and pronoun preference for an individual.
>
> **Physical markers:** Aspects of the human body that are considered to determine sex and/or gender for a given culture or society, including genitalia, chromosomes, hormones, secondary sex characteristics, and internal reproductive organs.
>
> **Gender expression and cues:** Aspects of behavior and outward presentation that may (intentionally or unintentionally) communicate gender to others in a given culture or society, including clothing, body language, hairstyles, socialization, interests, and presence in gendered spaces (e.g., restrooms, places of worship). Refers to the manner in which a person

expresses gender through clothing, appearance, behavior, speech, etc. A person's gender expression may vary from the gender norms traditionally associated with that person's biological sex. Gender expression is separate from gender identity and sexual orientation.

Gender binary: The cultural expectation that there are only two sexes/genders—male and female—and that they are the opposite of each other.

Gender dysphoria (GD), formerly known as gender identity disorder (GID): This is the formal diagnosis for transgender identity in the *Diagnostic and Statistical Manual,* fifth edition (DSM 5). The criteria for GD are: a marked incongruence between one's experienced/expressed gender and assigned gender, of at least six months' duration, as manifested by specific criteria. The condition is associated with clinically significant distress or impairment in social, school, occupational, or other important areas of functioning. The DSM 5 is used to assist trained clinicians in the diagnosis of their patients' mental disorders as part of a case formulation assessment that leads to a fully informed treatment plan for each individual.

Gender neutral: A term that describes something (usually a space, such as a bathroom, or clothing) that is not segregated by sex/gender.

Gender nonconforming (GNC): Having or being perceived to have gender characteristics and/or behaviors that do not conform to traditional or societal expectations. Gender nonconforming people may or may not identify as transgender. While GNC people are often assumed to be lesbian, gay, or bisexual, sexual orientation cannot be determined by a person's appearance or degree of gender conformity.

Gender norms: Culturally based expectations of how people should act based on their sex or gender (e.g., men are masculine, women are feminine).

Genderqueer: A term for people who do not identify with the gender binary terms that have traditionally described gender identity (e.g., male/female, man/woman). *Also see* Gender nonconforming and Transgender.

Gender roles: Social and cultural beliefs about what is considered gender-appropriate behavior, and the ways that men and women are expected to act.

Intersex/disorders of sex development (DSD): A label used to describe a person whose combination of chromosomes, gonads, hormones, and/or genitals differs from one of the two expected patterns of male or female. Up to 1 in 1,000 births may be considered to be intersex, meaning that the child's combination of chromosomes, gonads, or hormones present in a way that is not strictly male or female. Intersex/DSD is a group of chromosomal, genital, and hormonal disorders of sex development (DSD) and is distinct from transgender. Note: this term replaces "hermaphrodite," which is considered offensive.

LGBTQ: An acronym commonly used to refer to lesbian, gay, bisexual, transgender, and questioning individuals and communities. LGBTQ is often erroneously used as a synonym for "nonheterosexual," which incorrectly assumes that transgender is a sexual orientation.

Medical transition: A long-term process that utilizes hormonal treatments and/or surgical interventions to bring a person's body into congruence with that person's gender identity. Many, but not all, transgender people desire to transition medically.

MTF/male-to-female: *See* Transgender women and girls.

Pansexual: An identity label used to describe a sexual orientation based on attraction to people, rather than to a specific sex or gender.

Preferred gender pronouns: The ways that people refer to themselves and how they prefer to be referred to in terms of gender. Also referred to as pronoun preference or PGPs. The most common preferred gender pronouns are:

- She/her/hers: "She wants to see her caseworker, and is in the waiting room."
- He/him/his: "He has a meeting with his court-appointed lawyer this afternoon."
- Zie or Ze/hir/hirs (sounds like "zee," "here," and "heres"): "Ze has an appointment with hir dentist for next week."

Pubertal suppression: A medical process that "pauses" the hormonal changes that instigate puberty in young adolescents, resulting in a purposeful delay of the development of secondary sex characteristics (e.g., breast growth, testicular enlargement, facial hair, body fat redistribution, voice changes). Suppression allows time for further psychological development and can prevent the increased gender dysphoria that often accompanies puberty for transgender or gender noncomforming (TGNC) youth.

Questioning: Refers to people, often adolescents, who are exploring or questioning their gender identity or expression. Some may later identify as transgender or gender nonconforming, while others will not. This can also refer to people who are questioning their sexual orientation.

Resilience: Refers to the capacity to recover quickly from difficulties, or the ability to become strong, healthy, or successful again after adversity. This term is often used to describe transgender and gender nonconforming people, who despite experiencing extreme discrimination, harassment, and violence in all aspects of their lives, have the ability to cope and overcome these significant barriers.

Sexual orientation: Refers to a person's emotional, psychological, physical, and sexual attraction toward other people of the same or different gender. Sexual orientation is separate and distinct from gender identity and gender expression. Sexual orientation is about attraction to other people (external), while gender identity is a deep-seated sense of self (internal).

Social transition: The process of disclosing to oneself and others that one is transgender. This often includes asking that others use a name, pronoun, or gender that is more congruent with that person's gender identity.

Transgender communities: Transgender is also used as an umbrella term to refer to the communities of people that include all whose gender identity or gender expression does not match society's expectations of how individuals should behave in relation to their gender (e.g. transsexual, transgender, genderqueer, gender nonconforming, and other people whose gender expressions vary from traditional gender norms).

Transgender health care: Broadly describes the medical care that some transgender, transsexual, and gender nonconforming people seek in relation to their gender identity. The term may be used in specific instances to describe specific types of care, which may include supportive psychotherapy, hormonal therapies, surgical procedures, voice therapy, and/or electrolysis/laser hair removal.

Transgender men and boys: People who identify as male but were assigned female at birth. Similarly, the terms FTM or female-to-male refer to those who now identify as boys or men.

Transgender person: A term for a person whose gender identity (internal sense of self) is incongruent with that person's biological sex (physical body). Note: it is inappropriate and can be considered offensive to add an "ed" or "s" to the word (i.e., transgendered or transgenders).

Transgender women and girls: People who identify as female but were assigned male at birth. Similarly, the terms MTF or male-to-female refer to those who now identify as girls or women.

Transphobia: A negative, derogatory, prejudicial, or discriminatory response to a person who is (or is perceived to be) transgender or gender nonconforming.

Transsexual: A term that is sometimes used to refer to a transgender person who has engaged in a medical transition from one sex/gender to another, so that the person's body and gender identity are more physically aligned with their gender identity.

Two-spirit: An identity label used by indigenous North Americans to indicate that they embody both a masculine and feminine spirit. May also be used to include native peoples of diverse sexual orientations, and has different nuanced meanings in different native subcultures.

WPATH Standards of Care: The standards of care provide guidance for TGNC-affirming medical and mental health providers in determining if and when a person is ready/able to engage in medical interventions such as pubertal suppression, hormonal treatments, and/or surgeries. The standards of care are available online at: wpath.org/publications_standards.cf.

ACKNOWLEDGMENTS

My biggest thanks goes to Erin Leddy, for helping me through every step of writing this book. Whenever I was lost on the writing trail, you were always there with fresh perspective, new ideas, and alternate routes. I am grateful for your editing, research, feedback, guidance, honesty, and willingness to weed through all my random tangents and thoughts. I am grateful to have the opportunity to work with such a smart, thoughtful person throughout this process. Jill and Erika told me you were amazing before we even started, and they were right.

Thank you, Jill Friedlander and Erika Heilman. From the first time we chatted on the phone, I knew I should get on board with you two amazing women. I am so grateful for the opportunity to write about this message. Thank you for bringing together such a welcoming team of interesting authors and staff at Bibliomotion, Inc. And thank you for trusting in me even when I confessed that I wasn't entirely sure that I would finish writing the first book, much less consider writing another. I have a whole new standard of what can be done, thanks to you.

Huge thanks to my dear friend Vicki Hoefle, for connecting me with Bibliomotion, Inc. Bruce and I cherish our time with you, digging in deep as well as finding the humor in it all. We feast on your parenting wisdom every step of the way. You keep us reaching for more connection with our kids. Looking forward to your upcoming book.

Thank you, Susan Lauzau. You taught me a lot through our first round. Your cognitive retention is off the charts. I am impressed by your patience and grateful for how you help me get sorted and organized. You ask great questions and always nudge me in the right direction.

Thank you to Jill Schoenhaut for helping me lock up the details and make this presentable. Your patience with my questions and limitations is above and beyond.

Thank you to the Bibliomotion team: Shevaun Betzler, Ari Choquette, Alicia Simons, and David Ullmann. You are a sharp, savvy team!

Thank you to Maggie Goldstein Cooper for being my West Coast connector and for brainstorming great ways to move this message forward. You are the best!

Thank you, Dr. Mary Bender, for directing me to helpful resources and current research. The world needs a birth control enthusiast like you!

Thanks to my generous contributors: Eric Barthold, Loren Cannon, Mike Domitrz, Andrew Goldstein, Dr. Jim Hopper, Shana Natelson, Rhodes Perry, Jessica Pettitt, Sharyn Potter, Josiah Proietti, Jane Stapleton, Mark Tappan, Kaylee Wolfe, and Mike Wooten.

Thanks to this group of experts and mentors for engaging in conversations and helping me expand my understanding: Eric Barthold, Dr. Mary Bender, Marianne Bocock Doyle, Barnes Bofffey, Sarah Callaway, Dr. Steve Chapman, Annie E. Clark, David Cook, Amie Creagh, Lucia Gagliardone, Maggie Goldstein Cooper, Kevin Gallagher, Nancy Gaynor, Connor Gibson, Chad Green, Dr. Jill Grimes, Nicole Hager, Dr. Caroline Heldman, Dr. Jim Hopper, Jonathan Kalin, Jennifer Lagor, Mary Liscinsky, Michael Livingston, Dr. Michael Lyons, Leah McLaughry, Sabina McMahon, Shana Natelson, Kevin O'Brien, William Okin, Sohier Perry, Jessica Pettitt, Josiah Proietti, Brook Raney, Susanne Schmidt, Dr. Cathy Schubkin, Robbie Tanner, Mark Tappan, Edie

Thys Morgan, Sam Van Wetter, Al Vernacchio, Kaylee Wolfe, Mike Wooten, and Christa Wurm.

Thank you, Jessica Pettitt, for educating me with patience, humor, and understanding just the way you do with every person who has the privilege of sitting in your audience. The mentorship and encouragement you give so generously have also helped the careers of many other speakers. Thanks for many big laughs. Keep spreading wisdom through Good Enough Now and I Am Social Justice.

Thank you, Walter Ford Jenkins, for trying to engage others in my message. You are a kind, good friend. On behalf of the Freshman Camp crew, we consider you to be one of the finest people we know, and your presence in our lives is a blessing. Keep on rolling, wagon wheels.

Thank you, Mike O'Malley, for regularly dropping this wisdom bomb over the last few decades: "College is the only time you will be a five minute walk from twenty-five of your closest friends." It is impressive how you, the busiest friend is the one who inspires us to stop making busy and get together.

Thank you, Liza Bernard and Penny McConnel, of the Norwich Bookstore in Norwich, Vermont. Your support over the years has helped me spread my message. Working with you has been amazing. Your store has a very special vibe with an amazing team who lead so many Upper Valley folks to great literature. You spread joy through books and by creating community in your wonderful store.

Thanks to the Coven: Kristin Brown, Jane Esselstyn, Elizabeth Keene, and Pennie Rand. You lassies keep me grounded. Slainte Mhath.

Thanks to Lynn Pierce. When you joined our family, it got a whole lot more fun and way more interesting. Thank you for teaching me to find humor rather than shame in all of what life serves up. That skill led me to my life's purpose.

Thanks to my mom, Nancy Crawford Pierce, for showing me what social courage looks like. Watching you speak your mind and confront people who are mean, unfair, or rude shows us all that it is possible to get to the other side of awkward.

Big love to our children, Zander, Sadie, and Colter. You bless my world with your great minds and humor. Parenting you is a delight in and between the inevitable snags and tweaks, which tend to get funnier over time. The grace with which you handle having a social liability of a mom who squawks about sex in public is above and beyond. It may take a decade or three, but one day you will appreciate the outrageous conversations we stumble into regularly. Stay true to yourselves as the wind picks up! I love you all.

My deepest gratitude and love go to my husband, Bruce. Thank you for your unending support in this message and ongoing promotion. Thank you for running Pierce's Inn, shuffling kids, and keeping the chains moving down the field for our family while I am on the road speaking. Your ability to find and make humor in the oddest corners of life is a gift to our families and friends. You make me laugh every day. I love you.

NOTES

Chapter 1

1. "Articles and Advice," Dove Campaign for Real Beauty, The Real Truth About Beauty: Revisited, 2011, accessed March 9, 2016, http://www.dove.us/Social-Mission/campaign-for-real-beauty.aspx.

2. Caroline Heldman, "The Sexy Lie," TEDxYouth@SanDiego, San Diego, January 20, 2013. https://www.youtube.com/watch?v=kMS4VJKekW8.

3. C. Santos, K. Galligan, E. Pahlke, and R. Fabes, "Gender-Typed Behaviors, Achievement, and Adjustment Among Racially and Ethnically Diverse Boys During Early Adolescence," *American Journal of Orthopsychiatry* 83 (2013): 252–264.

4. E. Debold, L. M. Brown, S. Weseen, and G. K. Brookins, "Cultivating Hardiness Zones for Adolescent Girls: A Reconceptualization of Resilience in Relationships with Caring Adults, in *Beyond Appearances: A New Look at Adolescent Girls*, eds. N. Johnson, M. Roberts, and J. Worell (Washington, D.C.: American Psychological Association).

5. Kevan R. Wylie and Ian Eardley, "Penile Size and the 'Small Penis Syndrome,'" *BJU International* 99.6 (2007): 1449–1455, http://web.a.ebscohost.com.ezproxy.bowdoin.edu/ehost/pdfviewer/pdfviewer?sid=86feb34c-78cd-49e5-a06b-9f76566ebe27%40sessionmgr4002&vid=1&hid=4106.

6. Wylie and Eardley, "Penile Size," 1449–1455.

7. Wylie and Eardley, "Penile Size," 1449–1455.

8. Wyatt Myers, "Young Men Get Erectile Dysfunction, Too," *Everyday Health,* updated November 2, 2015, accessed May 7, 2015, http://www.everydayhealth.com/erectile-dysfunction/young-men-get-erectile-dysfunction-too.aspx.

9. Myers, "Young Men Get Erectile Dysfunction, Too."

10. "Evolution Has Not Prepared Your Brain for Today's Internet Porn," Your Brain on Porn, accessed December 23, 2015, http://brain1623.rssing.com/chan-10097734/all_p35.html.

11. Tyger Latham, "Does Porn Contribute to ED?" *Psychology Today,* May 3, 2012, accessed February 25, 2016, https://www.psychologytoday.com/blog/therapy-matters/201205/does-porn-contribute-ed.

12. Alexis E. Te, Darius A. Paduch, James A. Kashanian, Bilai Chughtai, and Richard Lee, *How Erections Work,* Weill Cornell Medical College James Buchanan Brady Foundation Department of Urology, accessed February 25, 2016, https://www.cornellurology.com/clinical-conditions/erectile-dysfunction/how-erections-work/.

13. Rosalind Wiseman, *Masterminds and Wingmen: Helping Your Son Cope with Schoolyard Power, Locker-Room Tests, Girlfriends, and the New Rules of Boy World* (New York: Harmony Books, 2013), 14.

14. J. Lloyd, N. S. Crouch, C. L. Minto, L.-M. Liao, and S. M. Creighton, "Female Genital Appearance: 'Normality' Unfolds," *BJOG: An International Journal of Obstetrics & Gynaecology* 112 (2005): 643–646, doi: 10.1111/j.1471-0528.2004.00517.x.

15. "About," The Great Wall of Vagina, accessed December 23, 2015, http://www.greatwallofvagina.co.uk/about.

16. Heldman, "The Sexy Lie."

Chapter 2

1. Frances Jensen, interview by Terry Gross, "Why Teens Are Impulsive, Addiction-Prone and Should Protect Their Brains," *Fresh Air,* National Public Radio, January 28, 2015, accessed February 15, 2015, http://www.npr.org/blogs/health/2015/01/28/381622350/why-teens-are-impulsive-addiction-prone-and-should-protect-their-brains.

2. Jensen, "Why Teens Are Impulsive."

3. Jensen, "Why Teens Are Impulsive."

4. Uhls, *Media Moms & Digital Dads,* 45.

5. Uhls, *Media Moms & Digital Dads,* 47.

6. Minas Michikyan, Jordan Morris, Debra Garcia, Gary W. Small, Eleni Zgourou, and Patricia M. Greenfield, "Five Days at Outdoor Education Camp Without Screens Improves Preteen Skills with Nonverbal Emotion Cues," *Computers in Human Behavior,* October, 2014, accessed November 4, 2015, http://www.sciencedirect.com/science/article/pii/S0747563214003227.

7. Michikyan, et al., "Five Days at Outdoor Education Camp."

8. Clifford Nass, interview by Ira Flatow, "The Myth of Multitasking," *Science Friday*, National Public Radio, May 10, 2013, accessed December 29, 2014, http://www.npr.org/2013/05/10/182861382/the-myth-of-multitasking.

9. Travis Bradberry, "Multitasking Damages Your Brain and Career, New Studies Suggest," *Forbes*, October 8, 2014, accessed February 24, 2015, http://www.forbes.com/sites/travisbradberry/2014/10/08/multitasking-damages-your-brain-and-career-new-studies-suggest/.

10. Catherine Steiner-Adair and Theresa H. Barker, *The Big Disconnect: Protecting Childhood and Family Relationships in the Digital Age* (New York: HarperCollins Publishers, 2014), 4.

11. Aziz Ansari and Eric Klinenberg, *Modern Romance* (New York: Penguin Press, 2015), 44.

12. Ansari and Klinenberg, *Modern Romance*, 41.

13. Sherry Turkle, *Reclaiming Conversation: The Power of Talk in a Digital Age,* (New York: Penguin Press), 22–23.

14. *Stop the Presses! Our Gay Dating App Survey Results Are In,* Grabhim.net, accessed February 27, 2016. http://grabhim.net/2015/03/17/stop-the-press es-our-gay-dating-app-survey-results-are-in/.

15. Mike Alvear, "83 Percent of Gay Men Have Sent a Dick Pic on Dating Apps, Says Survey," *Huffington Post*, March 18, 2015, accessed December 18, 2015, http://www.huffingtonpost.com/mike-alvear/83-percent-of-gay -men-send-dick-pics-on-dating-apps-says-survey_b_6893316.html.

16. Austin Tedesco, "BC Students Read Offensive Yik Yak Posts," *The Heights* blog, May 6, 2014, accessed February 28, 2016, http://bcheights .com/blog/2014/bc-students-read-offensive-yik-yak-posts/.

17. Austin Tedesco, "BC Students Read Offensive Yik Yak Posts," *The Heights* blog, May 6, 2014, accessed March 1, 2015, http://bcheights.com/blog/ 2014/bc-students-read-offensive-yik-yak-posts/.

Chapter 3

1. Gunilla Norris, *Inviting Silence* (Katonah, NY: Bluebridge, 2004), 7.

2. Sherry Turkle, *Reclaiming Conversation: The Power of Talk in a Digital Age* (Penguin Press, New York, 2015), 25.

3. Nancy Jo Sales, *American Girls: Social Media and the Secret Lives of Teenagers,* (New York: Alfred A. Knopf, 2016) 373.

4. "About the Film," webpage for *Race to Nowhere: The Dark Side of America's Achievement Culture*, Vicki Abeles and Jessica Congdon, codirectors, March 27, 2015, http://www.racetonowhere.com/about-film.

5. Roko Belic, "The Search for Happiness," *Huffington Post*, updated March 21, 2012, accessed January 27, 2015, http://www.huffingtonpost.com/roko-belic/happy-documentary_b_1220111.html.

6. Lisa M. Schab, *The Anxiety Workbook for Teens* (Oakland, CA: Instant Help Books, Harbinger Publications, 2008), 1.

Chapter 4

1. Frances Jensen, interview by Terry Gross, "Why Teens Are Impulsive, Addiction-Prone and Should Protect their Brains," *Fresh Air*, National Public Radio, January 28, 2015, accessed February 15, 2015. http://www.npr.org/sections/health-shots/2015/01/28/381622350/why-teens-are-impulsive-addiction-prone-and-should-protect-their-brains.

2. Alexandra Katehakis, "Effects of Porn on Adolescent Boys," *Psychology Today*, July 28, 2011, accessed March 26, 2015, https://www.psychologytoday.com/blog/sex-lies-trauma/201107/effects-porn-adolescent-boys.

3. "Brain Structure and Functional Connectivity Associated with Pornography Consumption: The Brain on Porn," Your Brain on Porn, August 16, 2014, accessed December 22, 2015, http://yourbrainonporn.com/brain-structure-and-functional-connectivity-associated-pornography-consumption-2014.

4. Sue Minto, "ChildLine Porn Campaign Confronts Issue of Young People and Porn," NSPCC, March 31, 2015, accessed November 1, 2015, https://www.nspcc.org.uk/fighting-for-childhood/news-opinion/sue-minto-we-cannot-shy-away-talking-about-porn/.

5. David Horsey, "Internet Porn Is an Experiment in Dehumanization," *Los Angeles Times*, December 15, 2014, accessed January 10, 2015, http://www.latimes.com/opinion/topoftheticket/la-na-tt-internet-porn-20141215-story.html.

6. Enough Is Enough, "Internet Safety 101: Pornography Statistics," April 28, 2014, accessed February 12, 2015, http://www.internetsafety101.org/Pornographystatistics.htm.

7. Gail Dines, *Pornland: How Porn Has Hijacked Our Sexuality* (Boston: Beacon Press, 2010), xxvi.

8. Dines, *Pornland*, xxvi.

9. Regan McMahon, "Porn Destroys Relationships, Lives," *SFGate, San Francisco Chronicle*, February 2, 2010, accessed December 27, 2014, http://www.sfgate.com/health/article/Porn-addiction-destroys-relationships-lives-3272230.php.

10. "Brain Studies on Porn Users," Your Brain On Porn, July 31, 2014, accessed December 23, 2015, http://yourbrainonporn.com/brain-scan-studies-porn -users.

11. Sales, *American Girls*, 373.

12. Maura Kelly, "The Rise of Anal Sex," *Marie Clare*, October 7, 2010, accessed February 25, 2015, http://www.marieclaire.com/sex-love/a5489/ rise-in-anal-sex-statistics/.

13. Katehakis, "Effects of Porn."

Chapter 5

1. Dr. Marty Klein, "Want to Watch a Lot of Porn AND Have Good Sex?," *Sexual Intelligence* blog, November 11, 2014, accessed December 15, 2014, https://sexualintelligence.wordpress.com/2014/11/11/want-to-watch -a-lot-of-porn-and-have-good-sex/.

2. Al Vernacchio, *For Goodness Sex: Changing the Way WE Talk to Teens About Sexuality, Values, and Health* (New York: HarperCollins, 2014), 191.

3. Sales, *American Girls,* 375.

4. Donna Freitas, *The End of Sex: How Hookup Culture Is Leaving a Generation Unhappy, Sexually Unfulfilled, and Confused About Intimacy* (New York: Basic Books, 2013), 112.

5. Vernacchio, *For Goodness Sex,* 158.

6. Freitas, *The End of Sex,* 112.

7. Lauren Kern and Malone Noreen, "Sex on Campus: The Politics of Hook-ups, Genders, 'Yes,'" *New York*, October 19, 2015, 32.

Chapter 6

1. Frances Jensen, interview by Terry Gross, "Why Teens Are Impulsive, Addiction-Prone and Should Protect Their Brains," *Fresh Air,* January 30, 2015, accessed February 28, 2015, http://www.npr.org/player/v2/media Player.html?action=1&t=1&islist=false&id=381622350&m=382175999.

2. Jensen, "Why Teens Are Impulsive."

3. Social Development Research Group/Seattle Children's Hospital, *A Parent's Guide to Preventing Underage Marijuana Use* (Seattle: Seattle Children's Hospital, 2014), 2, accessed March 2, 2015, http://learnaboutmarijuanawa .org/parentpreventionbooklet2014.pdf.

4. William Brangham, "Is Pot Getting More Potent?," *PBS Newshour* online, April 2, 2014, accessed March 1, 2015, http://www.pbs.org/newshour/ updates/pot-getting-potent/.

5. David. G. Newman, "Cannabis and Its Effects on Pilot Performance and Flight Safety: A Review," released in accordance with s.25 of the Transport Safety Investigation Act, 2003, 8-10, accessed February 2015, http://www.northstarbehavioral.com/Cannabis%20and%20its%20Effects%20on%20Pilot%20Performance%20and%20Flight%20Safety%20%28Australian%20Transportation%20Safety%20Bureau%202004%29%20%281%29.pdf.

6. National Institute of Drug Abuse, "Is Marijuana Addictive?," updated April 2015, accessed April 3, 2015, http://www.drugabuse.gov/publications/research-reports/marijuana/marijuana-addictive.

7. National Institute on Alcohol Abuse and Alcoholism, "College Drinking," July 2013, accessed April 3, 2015, http://pubs.niaaa.nih.gov/publications/CollegeFactSheet/CollegeFactSheet.pdf.

8. Student Health Services University of Pennsylvania, "Alcohol," 2015, accessed April 3, 2015, http://www.vpul.upenn.edu/shs/alcohol.php.

9. Elissa R. Weitzman, Toben F. Nelson, and Henry Wechsler, "Taking Up Binge Drinking in College: The Influences of Person, Social Group, and Environment," *Journal of Adolescent Health* (2003): 29, accessed April 3, 2015, http://archive.sph.harvard.edu/cas/Documents/uptake/uptake1.pdf.

10. Linda Thrasybule, "Pre-Gaming Risky for Young Adults," *Livescience*, November 9, 2012, accessed February 28, 2015, http://www.livescience.com/36730-pre-gaming-alcohol-risky-young-adults.html.

11. Student Health Services University of Pennsylvania, "Alcohol."

Chapter 7

1. The White House Task Force to Protect Students from Sexual Assault, comp, *Not Alone: The First Report of the White House Task Force to Protect Students from Sexual Assault*, 2014, 6, accessed October 1, 2015, https://www.whitehouse.gov/sites/default/files/docs/report_0.pdf.

2. *Not Alone*, vii.

3. David Lisak and Paul M. Miller, "Repeat Rape and Multiple Offending Among Undetected Rapists," *Violence and Victims* 17, no. 1 (2002), accessed March 11, 2016, http://www.davidlisak.com/wp-content/uploads/pdf/RepeatRapeinUndetectedRapists.pdf.

4. *Not Alone*, viii.

5. Christopher P. Krebs, Christine H. Lindquist, Tara D. Warner, Bonnie S. Fisher, and Sandra L. Martin, "The Campus Sexual Assault (CSA) Study: Final Report," prepared for the National Institute of Justice, 2007, viii,

accessed October 1, 2015, https://www.ncjrs.gov/app/abstractdb/Abstract DBDetails.aspx?id=243011.

6. Krebs, et al., "The Campus Sexual Assault Study," xiii.

7. Jaime M. Grant, Lisa A. Mottet, Justin Tanis, Jack Harrison, Jody L. Herman, and Mara Keisling, *Injustice at Every Turn: A Report of the National Transgender Discrimination Survey*, National Center for Transgender Equality and National Gay and Lesbian Task Force, 2011, 2, http://www.thetas kforce.org/static_html/downloads/reports/reports/ntds_full.pdf.

8. "NISVS: An Overview of 2010 Findings on Victimization by Sexual Orientation," The National Intimate Partner and Sexual Violence Survey, 2010, 1, accessed October 15, 2015, http://www.cdc.gov/violenceprevention/pdf/ cdc_nisvs_victimization_final-a.pdf.

9. Hayley Munguia, "Transgender Students Are Particularly Vulnerable to Campus Sexual Assault," *FiveThirtyEight: Life*, September 22, 2015, accessed December 22, 2015, http://fivethirtyeight.com/datalab/transgender-stude nts-are-particularly-vulnerable-to-campus-sexual-assault/.

10. E. Rothman, D. Exner, and A. L. Baughman, "The Prevalence of Sexual Assault Against People Who Identify As Gay, Lesbian or Bisexual in the United States: A Systematic Review," *Trauma, Violence, & Abuse* 12, no. 2 (2011): 55–66.

11. "NISVS: An Overview of 2010 Findings on Victimization by Sexual Orientation," The National Intimate Partner and Sexual Violence Survey, 2010.

12. Richard Pérez-Peña, "1 in 4 Women Experience Sex Assault on Campus," *New York Times*, September 21, 2015, accessed December 22, 2015, http://www .nytimes.com/2015/09/22/us/a-third-of-college-women-experience-unwante d-sexual-contact-study-finds.html?_r=1.

13. "Statistics," Rape, Abuse & Incest National Network, 2009, accessed March 2, 2016, https://rainn.org/statistics.

14. Jon Krakauer, *Missoula: Rape and the Justice System in a College Town* (New York: Doubleday, 2015), 253.

15. Krakauer, *Missoula*, 253–54.

16. Krakauer, *Missoula*, 254–55.

17. Krakauer, *Missoula*, 255.

18. Jim Hopper, "Neurobiology of Trauma and Sexual Assault," YouTube, July 24, 2015, accessed March 9, 2016, https://www.youtube.com/watch?v =dwTQ_U3p5Wc.

19. Senate Bill 967, Chapter 748, California Legislative Information, DB-967 Student Safety: Sexual Assault (2013–2014), accessed March 3, 2016,

https://leginfo.legislature.ca.gov/faces/billNavClient.xhtml?bill_id=201320140SB967.

20. Senate Bill 967, Chapter 748.

21. Al Vernacchio, interview by Steve Inskeep, "How Much Do Teenagers Know About Sex and the Law?," *Morning Edition,* NPR, September 3, 2015, http://www.npr.org/2015/09/03/437132828/how-much-do-teenagers-know-about-sex-and-the-law.

22. Katie Van Syckle, "Hooking Up Is Easy to Do (But Pretty Complicated)," *New York*, October 18, 2015.

Chapter 8

1. Jane Ward, "It Turns Out Male Sexuality Is Just As Fluid As Female Sexuality," *The Conversation*, February 2, 2015, accessed November 2, 2015, https://theconversation.com/it-turns-out-male-sexuality-is-just-as-fluid-as-female-sexuality-36189.

2. Ward, "It Turns Out."

3. Lauren Kern and Noreen Malone, "Sex on Campus: The Politics of Hookups, Genders, 'Yes,' " *New York*, October 19, 2015, 32.

4. "About the Program on Intergroup Relations," Program on Intergroup Relations, University of Michigan, 2016, accessed March 7, 2016, https://igr.umich.edu/about.

5. "Skidmore College Is the First College or University in the United States to Offer a Minor in Intergroup Relations," Intergroup Relations, Skidmore College, accessed March 7, 2016, http://www.skidmore.edu/igr/.

6. Lee Che Leong, "Testimony: NYC DOE Must Provide Comprehensive Sex Education," NYCLU, n.d., accessed March 24, 2015, http://www.nyclu.org/content/testimony-nyc-doe-must-provide-comprehensive-sex-education.

7. "Suicide Risk and Prevention for Lesbian, Gay, Bisexual, and Transgender Youth," Suicide Prevention Resource Center, Newton, MA, U.S. Department of Health and Human Resources, 2008, accessed March 4, 2016, http://www.sprc.org/sites/sprc.org/files/library/SPRC_LGBT_Youth.pdf.

8. Ric Chollar, "10 Physical and Emotional Health Concerns of LGBTQ Students," *Campus Pride*, June 17, 2013, accessed December 18, 2015, https://www.campuspride.org/resources/10-physical-and-emotional-health-concerns-of-lgbt-students/.

9. Emily A. Greytak, Joseph G. Kosciw, and Elizabeth M. Diaz, "Harsh Realities: The Experience of Transgender Youth in Our Nation's Schools," GLSEN, 2009, accessed March 8, 2016, http://www.glsen.org/sites/default/files/Harsh%20Realities.pdf.

Chapter 9

1. Anthony Bowlses, "Matthew Hussey Speaks on Behalf of Trojan to Encourage Safe Sex Practices," Examiner.com, September 25, 2014, accessed March 10, 2016, http://www.examiner.com/article/matthew-hussey-speaks-on-behalf-of-trojan-to-encourages-safe-sex-practices.

2. Laura Berman, "STDs in College: What Students Need to Know," Dr. Laura Berman on Love & Sex, *Everyday Health*, May 16, 2013, accessed December 20, 2015, http://www.everydayhealth.com/columns/dr-laura-berman-on-love-and-sex/stds-in-college-what-students-need-to-know/.

3. "STI General Information," Brown University Health Promotion: Answers to Questions You Have Always Wanted to Ask, accessed December 20, 2015, http://www.brown.edu/Student_Services/Health_Services/Health_Education/sexual_health/sexually_transmitted_infections/.

4. "College Health and Safety," August 18, 2015, accessed December 20, 2015, http://www.cdc.gov/family/college/.

5. "Globally, an Estimated Two-Thirds of the Population Under 50 Are Infected with Herpes Simplex Virus Type 1," World Health Organization Media Centre, 2015, accessed December 20, 2015, http://who.int/mediacentre/news/releases/2015/herpes/en/.

6. "Globally, an Estimated Two-Thirds of the Population Under 50 Are Infected with Herpes Simplex Virus Type 1," World Health Organization.

7. "Globally, an Estimated Two-Thirds of the Population Under 50 Are Infected with Herpes Simplex Virus Type 1," World Health Organization.

8. "2014 Sexually Transmitted Diseases Surveillance: Herpes Simplex Virus," Centers for Disease Control and Prevention, November 17, 2015, accessed January 3, 2016, http://www.cdc.gov/std/stats14/other.htm#herpes.

9. Grimes MD, Jill, *Seductive Delusions: How Everyday People Get STDs*, (Baltimore, The Johns Hopkins University Press, 2008) 22.

10. Grimes, Seductive Delusions, 23.

11. "Herpes Simplex," The New York Times Health Guide, July 13, 2016, accessed July 13, 2016. http://www.nytimes.com/health/guides/disease/herpes-simplex/risk-factors.html

12. "What Is Chlamydia? STD Symptoms, Testing and Treatment," Planned Parenthood, 2014, accessed January 3, 2016, https://www.plannedparenthood.org/learn/stds-hiv-safer-sex/chlamydia.

13. "Gonorrhea—CDC Fact Sheet (Detailed Version)," Centers for Disease Control and Prevention, November 17, 2015, accessed January 3, 2016, http://www.cdc.gov/std/gonorrhea/stdfact-gonorrhea-detailed.htm.

14. "Crabs," ASHA: American Sexual Health Association, 2015, accessed December 30, 2015, http://www.ashasexualhealth.org/stdsstis/crabs/.

15. "Hepatitis B," World Health Organization Media Centre, July 1, 2015, accessed January 2, 2016, http://www.who.int/mediacentre/factsheets/fs204/en/.

16. "Stages of HIV Infection," AIDS.gov, U.S. Department of Health and Human Services, revised August 27, 2015, accessed March 7, 2016, https://www.aids.gov/hiv-aids-basics/just-diagnosed-with-hiv-aids/hiv-in-your-body/stages-of-hiv/.

17. "Basic Statistics," Centers for Disease Control and Prevention: HIV/AIDS, November 3, 2015, accessed January 2, 2016, http://www.cdc.gov/hiv/basics/statistics.html.

18. "What Is Truvada?," Truvada, Gilead corporate website, 2014, accessed March 12, 2016, http://www.truvada.com/treatment-for-hivDrugs.com.

19. "What Is Truvada?"

20. Lori Gawron, "Contraceptive Management and Updates," University of Utah School of Medicine, 2016, accessed March 12, 2016, http://utahafp.org/wp-content/uploads/2016/02/Contraceptive-Management-and-Updates.-Gawron.pdf.

21. *Effectiveness of Family Planning Methods*, Centers for Disease Control and Prevention, 2014, http://www.cdc.gov/reproductivehealth/Unintended Pregnancy/PDF/Family-Planning-Methods-2014.pdf.

Resources

1. "About the National Sexual Assault Telephone Hotline," RAINN (Rape, Abuse and Incest National Network), accessed December 22, 2015, https://www.rainn.org/get-help/national-sexual-assault-hotline.

2. *Campus SaVE Act, Guidebook—How to Exceed Campus SaVE (Clery Act) and Title IX Compliance*, 2014, accessed March 13, 2016, http://thecampussaveact.com/faq/.

3. "The Clery Act," End Rape on Campus, accessed December 22, 2015, http://endrapeoncampus.org/the-clery-act/.

4. "Defining Dating Violence," Michigan Domestic and Sexual Violence Prevention and Treatment Board, 2015, accessed December 22, 2015, http://www.michigan.gov/datingviolence/0,4559,7-233-46553-169521--,00.html.

5. Christopher P. Krebs, Christine H. Lindquist, Tara D. Warner, Bonnie S. Fisher, and Sandra L. Martin, *The Campus Sexual Assault (CSA) Study: Final*

Report, prepared for the National Institute of Justice, 2007, 1–2, accessed October 1, 2015, https://www.ncjrs.gov/pdffiles1/nij/grants/221153.pdf.

6. "Sexual Assault Nurse Examiners," International Association of Forensic Nurses, 2015, accessed December 22, 2015, http://www.forensicnurses .org/?page=aboutsane.

7. "What Is a Rape Kit?" RAINN (Rape, Abuse and Incest National Network) Washington, D.C., 2009, accessed March 8, 2016, https://rainn. org/get-information/sexual-assault-recovery/rape-kit.

8. "Sexual Assault," U.S. Department of Justice, April 2, 2015, accessed December 22, 2015, http://www.justice.gov/ovw/sexual-assault.

9. *Statutory Rape: A Guide to State Laws and Reporting Requirements, Summary of Current State Laws*, ASPE: Office of the Assistant Secretary for Planning and Evaluation, 2004, accessed October 15, 2015, https://aspe.hhs.gov/ report/statutory-rape-guide-state-laws-and-reporting-requirements-summa ry-current-state-laws.

10. "Overview of Title IX of the Education Amendments of 1972, 20 U.S.C. AÂ§ 1681 Et. Seq.," U.S. Department of Justice, August 7, 2015, accessed December 18, 2015, http://www.justice.gov/crt/overview-title-ix-education -amendments-1972-20-usc-1681-et-seq.

11. "About Us," Prevention Innovations Research Center, accessed January 5, 2016, http://cola.unh.edu/prevention-innovations-research-center/ about-us.

12. J. R. Perry and E. R. Green, *Safe & Respected: Policy, Best Practices & Guidance for Serving Transgender & Gender Non-Conforming Children and Youth Involved in the Child Welfare, Detention, and Juvenile Justice Systems* (New York: New York City's Administration for Children's Services, 2014), 57–59.

REFERENCES

Abeles, Vicki, and Jessica Congdon, directors. "About the Film," *Race to Nowhere: The Dark Side of America's Achievement Culture.* March 27, 2015. http://www.racetonowhere.com/about-film.

Alvear, Mike. "83 Percent of Gay Men Have Sent a Dick Pic on Dating Apps, Says Survey." *Huffington Post*, March 18, 2015. Accessed December 18, 2015. http://www.huffingtonpost.com/mike-alvear/83-percent-of-gay-men -send-dick-pics-on-dating-apps-says-survey_b_6893316.html.

American Sexual Health Association. "Crabs." ASHA: American Sexual Health. Association, 2015. Accessed December 30, 2015. http://www.ashasexual health.org/stdsstis/crabs/.

Ansari, Aziz, and Eric Klinenberg. *Modern Romance.* New York: Penguin Press, 2015.

Belic, Roko. "The Search for Happiness." *Huffington Post*, updated March 21, 2012. Accessed January 27, 2015. http://www.huffingtonpost.com/roko -belic/happy-documentary_b_1220111.html.

Berman, Laura. "STDs in College: What Students Need to Know." Dr. Laura Berman on Love & Sex, *Everyday Health*, May 16, 2013. Accessed December 20, 2015. http://www.everydayhealth.com/columns/dr-laura -berman-on-love-and-sex/stds-in-college-what-students-need-to-know/.

Bowles, Anthony. "Matthew Hussey Speaks on Behalf of Trojan to Encourage Safe Sex Practices." Examiner.com, September 25, 2014. Accessed March 10, 2016. http://www.examiner.com/article/matthew-hussey-speaks -on-behalf-of-trojan-to-encourages-safe-sex-practices.

Bradberry, Travis. "Multitasking Damages Your Brain and Career, New Studies Suggest." *Forbes*, October 8, 2014. Accessed February 24, 2015. http:// www.forbes.com/sites/travisbradberry/2014/10/08/multitasking-damages- your-brain-and-career-new-studies-suggest/.

Brangham, William. "Is Pot Getting More Potent?" *PBS Newshour* online, April 2, 2014. Accessed March 1, 2015. http://www.pbs.org/newshour/updates/pot-getting-potent/.

Brown, L. M., E. Debold, S. Weseen, and G. K. Brookins. "Cultivating Hardiness Zones for Adolescent Girls: A Reconceptualization of Resilience in Relationships with Caring Adults." In *Beyond Appearances: A New Look at Adolescent Girls*, edited by N. Johnson, M. Roberts, and J. Worell. Washington, D.C.: American Psychological Association, 1999.

Brown University. "STI General Information." *Brown University Health Promotion: Answers to Questions You Have Always Wanted to Ask*. Accessed December 20, 2015. http://www.brown.edu/Student_Services/Health_Services/Health_Education/sexual_health/sexually_transmitted_infections/.

Centers for Disease Control and Prevention. "About HIV/AIDS." Centers for Disease Control and Prevention, December 6, 2015. Accessed January 2, 2016. http://www.cdc.gov/hiv/basics/whatishiv.html.

———. "Basic Statistics." Centers for Disease Control and Prevention, November 3, 2015. Accessed January 2, 2016. http://www.cdc.gov/hiv/basics/statistics.html.

———. "College Health and Safety." Centers for Disease Control and Prevention, August 18, 2015. Accessed December 20, 2015. http://www.cdc.gov/family/college/.

———. *Effectiveness of Family Planning Methods*. Centers for Disease Control and Prevention, 2014. Accessed February 1, 2016. http://www.cdc.gov/reproductivehealth/UnintendedPregnancy/PDF/Family-Planning-Methods-2014.pdf.

———. "Gonorrhea—CDC Fact Sheet (Detailed Version)." Centers for Disease Control and Prevention, November 17, 2015. Accessed January 3, 2016. http://www.cdc.gov/std/gonorrhea/stdfact-gonorrhea-detailed.htm.

———. "Hepatitis A: Questions and Answers for the Public." Centers for Disease Control and Prevention, December 22, 2015. Accessed December 30, 2015. http://www.cdc.gov/hepatitis/hav/afaq.htm#statistics.

———. "Hepatitis B: FAQs for Health Professionals." Centers for Disease Control and Prevention, December 16, 2015. Accessed January 3, 2016. http://www.cdc.gov/hepatitis/hbv/hbvfaq.htm#b6.

———. "Pubic 'Crab' Lice: Prevention & Control." Centers for Disease Control and Prevention, September 24, 2013. Accessed December 30, 2015. http://www.cdc.gov/parasites/lice/pubic/prevent.html.

———. "2014 Sexually Transmitted Diseases Surveillance: Herpes Simplex Virus," Centers for Disease Control and Prevention, November 17,

2015. Accessed January 3, 2016, http://www.cdc.gov/std/stats14/other.htm#herpes.

———. "Syphilis—CDC Fact Sheet." Centers for Disease Control and Prevention: Sexually Transmitted Diseases (STDs), November 12, 2015. Accessed December 30, 2015. http://www.cdc.gov/std/syphilis/stdfact-syphilis.htm.

———. "Viral Hepatitis—Hepatitis B Information." Centers for Disease Control and Prevention, May 31, 2015. Accessed December 30, 2015. http://www.cdc.gov/hepatitis/hbv/.

Chollar, Ric. "10 Physical and Emotional Health Concerns of LGBTQ Students." *Campus Pride,* June 17, 2013. Accessed December 18, 2015. https://www.campuspride.org/resources/10-physical-and-emotional-health-concerns-of-lgbt-students/.

Dines, Gail. *Pornland: How Porn Has Hijacked Our Sexuality.* Boston: Beacon Press, 2010.

End Rape on Campus. "The Clery Act." End Rape on Campus (EROC). Accessed December 22, 2015. http://endrapeoncampus.org/the-clery-act/.

Enough Is Enough. "Internet Safety 101: Pornography Statistics." April 28, 2014. Accessed February 12, 2015. http://www.internetsafety101.org/Pornographystatistics.htm.

EverFi, *Guidebook—How to Exceed Campus SaVE (Clery Act) and Title IX Compliance,* 2014. Accessed March 13, 2016. http://thecampussaveact.com/faq/.

Freitas, Donna. *The End of Sex: How Hookup Culture Is Leaving a Generation Unhappy, Sexually Unfulfilled, and Confused About Intimacy.* New York: Basic Books, 2013.

Gawron, Lori. "Contraceptive Management and Updates." University of Utah School of Medicine, 2016. Accessed March 12, 2016. http://health.gsu.edu/womens-health/contraceptive-mgt/.

Gilead Sciences. "What Is Truvada?" Truvada: Gilead corporate website, 2014. Accessed March 12, 2016. http://www.truvada.com/?utm_source=google&utm_medium=cpc&utm_campaign=dtp_b_truvada%20prep%20branded_desktop&utm_content=truvada%20general_%20phrase&utm_term=truvada&utm_moc=4621000030.

Glosser, Asaph, Karen Gardiner, and Mike Fishman. *Statutory Rape: A Guide to State Laws and Reporting Requirements, Summary of Current State Laws.* ASPE: Office of the Assistant Secretary for Planning and Evaluation. 2004. Accessed October 15, 2015. https://aspe.hhs.gov/report/statutory-rape-guide-state-laws-and-reporting-requirements-summary-current-state-laws.

GrabHim.net. "Stop the Presses! Our Gay Dating App Survey Results Are In!,"
February 2015. Accessed February 27, 2016. http://grabhim.net/2015/03/
17/stop-the-presses-our-gay-dating-app-survey-results-are-in/.

Grant, Jaime M., Lisa A. Mottet, Justin Tanis, Jack Harrison, Jody L. Herman,
and Mara Keisling. *Injustice at Every Turn: A Report of the National Transgender Discrimination Survey.* National Center for Transgender Equality
and National Gay and Lesbian Task Force, 2011. http://www.thetaskforce
.org/static_html/downloads/reports/reports/ntds_full.pdf.

Greytak, Emily A., Joseph G. Kosciq, and Elizabeth M. Diaz. "Harsh Realities:
The Experience of Transgender Youth in Our Nation's Schools." GLSEN,
2009. Accessed March 8, 2016. http://www.glsen.org/sites/default/files/
Harsh%20Realities.pdf.

Grimes, Jill. *Seductive Delusions: How Everyday People Catch STDs.* Baltimore,
MD: Johns Hopkins University Press, 2008.

Heldman, Caroline. "The Sexy Lie." TEDxYouth@SanDiego, January 20, 2013.
https://www.youtube.com/watch?v=kMS4VJKekW8.

Hopper, James. "Neurobiology of Trauma and Sexual Assault." YouTube,
July 24, 2015. Accessed March 9, 2016. https://www.youtube.com/
watch?v=dwTQ_U3p5Wc.

Horsey, David. "Internet Porn Is an Experiment in Dehumanization." *Los Angeles Times,* December 15, 2014. Accessed January 10, 2015. http://www.lat-
imes.com/opinion/topoftheticket/la-na-tt-internet-porn-20141215-story.
html.

International Association of Forensic Nurses. "Sexual Assault Nurse Examiners."
International Association of Forensic Nurses, 2015. Accessed December 22,
2015. http://www.forensicnurses.org/?page=aboutsane.

Jensen, Frances. "Why Teens Are Impulsive, Addiction-Prone, and Should Protect Their Brains." Interview by Terry Gross. *Fresh Air.* National Public
Radio, January 28, 2015. Accessed February 15, 2015. http://www.npr.org/
blogs/health/2015/01/28/381622350/why-teens-are-impulsive-addiction
-prone-and-should-protect-their-brains.

Katehakis, Alexandra. "Effects of Porn on Adolescent Boys." *Psychology Today,*
July 28, 2011. Accessed March 26, 2015. https://www.psychologytoday.
com/blog/sex-lies-trauma/201107/effects-porn-adolescent-boys.

Kelly, Maura. "The Rise of Anal Sex." *Marie Claire,* October 7, 2010.
Accessed February 25, 2015. http://www.marieclaire.com/sex-love/a5489/
rise-in-anal-sex-statistics/.

Kern, Lauren, and Malone Noreen. "Sex on Campus: The Politics of Hookups,
Genders, 'Yes.'" *New York,* October 19, 2015.

Klein, Marty. "Want to Watch a Lot of Porn AND Have Good Sex?" *Sexual Intelligence* blog, November 11, 2014. Accessed December 15, 2014. https://sexualintelligence.wordpress.com/2014/11/11/want-to-watch-a -lot-of-porn-and-have-good-sex/.

Krakauer, Jon. *Missoula: Rape and the Justice System in a College Town.* New York: Doubleday, 2015.

Krebs, Christopher P., Christine H. Lindquist, Tara D. Warner, Bonnie S. Fisher, and Sandra L. Martin. "The Campus Sexual Assault (CSA) Study: Final Report." Prepared for the National Institute of Justice, 2007. Accessed October 1, 2015. https://www.ncjrs.gov/app/abstractdb/AbstractDB-Details.aspx?id=243011 and https://www.ncjrs.gov/pdffiles1/nij/grants/221153.pdf.

Latham, Tyger. "Does Porn Contribute to ED?" *Psychology Today,* May 3, 2012. Accessed February 25, 2016. https://www.psychologytoday.com/blog/therapy-matters/201205/does-porn-contribute-ed.

Lisak, David, and Paul M. Miller. "Repeat Rape and Multiple Offending Among Undetected Rapists." *Violence and Victims* 17, no. 1, 2002. Accessed March 11, 2016. http://www.davidlisak.com/wpcontent/uploads/pdf/RepeatRapeinUndetectedRapists.pdf.

Lloyd, J., N. S. Crouch, C. L Minto, L. M. Liao, and S. M. Creighton. "Female Genital Appearance: 'Normality' Unfolds." *BJOG: An International Journal of Obstetrics & Gynaecology,* 2005. http://onlinelibrary.wiley.com/doi/10.1111/j.1471-0528.2004.00517.x/abstract.

McMahon, Regan. "Porn Destroys Relationships, Lives." *SFGate, San Francisco Chronicle,* online edition, February 2, 2010. Accessed December 27, 2014. http://www.sfgate.com/health/article/Porn-addiction-destroys-relationships -lives-3272230.php.

Michigan Domestic and Sexual Violence Prevention and Treatment Board. "Defining Dating Violence." Teen Dating Violence, 2015. Accessed December 22, 2015. http://www.michigan.gov/datingviolence/0,4559,7 -233-46553-169521--,00.html.

Minto, Sue. "ChildLine Porn Campaign Confronts Issue of Young People and Porn." NSPCC, March 31, 2015. Accessed November 1, 2015. https://www .nspcc.org.uk/fighting-for-childhood/news-opinion/sue-minto-we-cannot -shy-away-talking-about-porn/.

Munguia, Hayley. "Transgender Students Are Particularly Vulnerable to Campus Sexual Assault." *FiveThirtyEight: Life,* September 22, 2015. Accessed December 22, 2015. http://fivethirtyeight.com/datalab/transgender-students-are -particularly-vulnerable-to-campus-sexual-assault/.

Myers, Wyatt. "Young Men Get Erectile Dysfunction, Too." *Everyday Health,* updated November 2, 2015. Accessed May 7, 2015. http://www.everyday health.com/erectile-dysfunction/young-men-get-erectile-dysfunction-too .aspx.

Nass, Clifford. "The Myth of Multitasking." Interview by Ira Flatow. *Science Friday.* National Public Radio, May 10, 2013. Accessed December 29, 2014. http://www.npr.org/2013/05/10/182861382/the-myth-of-multitasking.

National Institute on Alcohol Abuse and Alcoholism. "College Drinking." National Institutes of Health, July 2013. Accessed April 3, 2015. http:// pubs.niaaa.nih.gov/publications/CollegeFactSheet/CollegeFactSheet.pdf.

National Institute of Drug Abuse. "Is Marijuana Addictive?" National Institutes of Health, updated April 2015. Accessed April 3, 2015. http://www.drugabuse .gov/publications/research-reports/marijuana/marijuana-addictive.

National Intimate Partner Sexual Violence Survey (NISVS). "An Overview of 2010 Findings on Victimization by Sexual Orientation." Centers for Disease Control and Prevention, 2010. Accessed October 15, 2015. http://www.cdc .gov/violenceprevention/pdf/cdc_nisvs_victimization_final-a.pdf.

Newman, David. G. "Cannabis and Its Effects on Pilot Performance and Flight Safety: A Review." Released in accordance with s.25 of the Transport Safety Investigation Act, 2003. Accessed February 2015. http://www.northstarbe havioral.com/Cannabis%20and%20its%20Effects%20on%20Pilot%20 Performance%20and%20Flight%20Safety%20%28Australian%20Trans portation%20Safety%20Bureau%202004%29%20%281%29.pdf.

Norris, Gunilla. *Inviting Silence.* Katonah, NY: Bluebridge, 2004.

NYCLU. "Testimony: NYC DOE Must Provide Comprehensive Sex Education." Testimony before the New York City Council Committee on Health, January 2, 2008. Accessed March 24, 2015. http://www.nyclu.org/ content/testimony-nyc-doe-must-provide-comprehensive-sex-education.

Pérez-Peña, Richard. "1 in 4 Women Experience Sex Assault on Campus." *New York Times,* September 21, 2015. Accessed December 22, 2015. http:// www.nytimes.com/2015/09/22/us/a-third-of-college-women-experience -unwanted-sexual-contact-study-finds.html?r=1.

Perry, J. R., and E. R. Green. *Safe & Respected: Policy, Best Practices & Guidance for Serving Transgender & Gender Non-Conforming Children and Youth Involved in the Child Welfare, Detention, and Juvenile Justice Systems.* New York: New York City's Administration for Children's Services, 2014.

Planned Parenthood. "What Is Chlamydia? STD Symptoms, Testing and Treatment." Planned Parenthood Federation of America, 2014. Accessed January 3, 2016. https://www.plannedparenthood.org/learn/stds-hiv-safer-sex/chlamydia

Prevention Innovations Research Center (PIRC). "Evidenced-Based Initiatives." University of New Hampshire College of Liberal Arts, 2016. Accessed January 5, 2016. http://cola.unh.edu/prevention-innovations-research-center/about-us.

RAINN. "About the National Sexual Assault Telephone Hotline." Rape, Abuse and Incest National Network (RAINN), 2009. Accessed December 22, 2015. https:// www.rainn.org/get-help/national-sexual-assault-hotline.

———. "What Is a Rape Kit?" Rape, Abuse and Incest National Network (RAINN), 2009. Accessed March 8, 2016. https://rainn.org/get-information/sexual-assault-recovery/rape-kit.

———. "Statistics." Rape, Abuse, and Incest National Network (RAINN), 2009. Accessed March 2, 2016. https://rainn.org/statistics.

Rothman, E., D. Exner, and A. L. Baughman. "The Prevalence of Sexual Assault Against People Who Identify As Gay, Lesbian or Bisexual in the United States: A Systematic Review." *Trauma, Violence, & Abuse,* 2011.

Sales, Nancy Jo. *American Girls: Social Media and the Secret Lives of Teenagers.* New York: Alfred Knopf, 2016.

Santos, C., K. Galligan, E. Pahlke, and R. Fabes. "Gender-Typed Behaviors, Achievement, and Adjustment Among Racially and Ethnically Diverse Boys During Early Adolescence." *American Journal of Orthopsychiatry,* 2013. http://www.ncbi.nlm.nih.gov/pubmed/23889017.

Schab, Lisa M. *The Anxiety Workbook for Teens.* Oakland, CA: Instant Help Books, Harbinger Publications, 2008.

Senate Bill 967, Chapter 748. California Legislative Information, DB-967. Student Safety: Sexual Assault, 2013–2014. Accessed March 3, 2016. https://leginfo.legislature.ca.gov/faces/billNavClient.xhtml?bill_id=201320140SB967.

Skidmore College. "Skidmore College Is the First College or University in the United States to Offer a Minor in Intergroup Relations." Intergroup Relations, Skidmore College. Accessed March 7, 2016. http://www.skidmore.edu/igr/.

Social Development Research Group/Seattle Children's Hospital. *A Parent's Guide to Preventing Underage Marijuana Use.* Seattle: Seattle Children's Hospital, 2014. Accessed March 2, 2015. http://learnaboutmarijuanawa.org/parentpreventionbooklet2014.pdf.

Steiner-Adair, Catherine, and Theresa H. Barker. *The Big Disconnect: Protecting Childhood and Family Relationships in the Digital Age.* New York: HarperCollins Publishers, 2014.

Student Health Services University of Pennsylvania. "Alcohol." Vice Provost for University Life (VPUL), 2015. Accessed April 3, 2015. http://www.vpul.upenn.edu/shs/alcohol.php.

Suicide Prevention Resource Center. *Suicide Risk and Prevention for Lesbian, Gay, Bisexual, and Transgender Youth.* Suicide Prevention Resource Center, 2008. Accessed March 4, 2016. http://www.sprc.org/sites/sprc.org/files/library/SPRC_LGBT_Youth.pdf

Te, Alexis E., Darius A. Paduch, James A. Kashanian, Bilai Chughtai, and Richard Lee. "How Erections Work." Weill Cornell Medical College James Buchanan Brady Foundation Department of Urology, 2001–16. Accessed February 25, 2016. https://www.cornellurology.com/clinical-conditions/erectile-dysfunction/how-erections-work/.

Tedesco, Austin. "BC Students Read Offensive Yik Yak Posts." *The Heights* blog, May 6, 2014. Accessed February 28, 2016. http://bcheights.com/blog/2014/bc-students-read-offensive-yik-yak-posts/.

Thrasybule, Linda. "Pre-Gaming Risky for Young Adults." *Livescience,* November 9, 2012. Accessed February 28, 2015. http://www.livescience.com/36730-pre-gaming-alcohol-risky-young-adults.html.

Turkle, Sherry. *Reclaiming Conversation: The Power of Talk in a Digital Age.* New York: Penguin Press, 2015.

———. "Stop Googling. Let's Talk." *New York Times*, September 26, 2015. http://www.nytimes.com/2015/09/27/opinion/sunday/stop-googling-lets-talk.html.

Unilever. "The Real Truth About Beauty: Revisited." The Dove Campaign for Real Beauty, 2011. http://www.dove.us/Social-Mission/campaign-for-real-beauty.aspx.

University of Michigan. "About the Program on Intergroup Relations." Program on Intergroup Relations, 2016. Accessed March 7, 2016. https://igr.umich.edu/about.

U.S. Department of Health and Human Services. "Stages of HIV Infection." AIDS.gov, revised August 27, 2015. Accessed March 7, 2016. https://www.aids.gov/hiv-aids-basics/just-diagnosed-with-hiv-aids/hiv-in-your-body/stages-of-hiv/.

U.S. Department of Justice. "Overview of Title IX of the Education Amendments of 1972, 20 U.S.C. AÂ§ 1681 Et. Seq." U.S. Department of Justice. August 7, 2015. Accessed December 18, 2015. http://www.justice.gov/crt/overview-title-ix-education-amendments-1972-20-usc-1681-et-seq.

———. "Sexual Assault." Office of Violence Against Women. April 2, 2015. Accessed December 22, 2015. https://www.justice.gov/ovw/sexual-assault.

Uhls, Yalda T. *Media Moms & Digital Dads.* Brookline, MA: Bibliomotion, Inc., 2015.

Uhls, Yalda, Minas Michikyan, Jordan Morris, Debra Garcia, Gary W. Small, Eleni Zgourou, Patricia M. Greenfield. "Five Days at Outdoor Education Camp Without Screens Improves Preteen Skills with Nonverbal Emotion Cues." *Computers in Human Behavior,* October 2014. Accessed November 4, 2015. http://www.sciencedirect.com/science/article/pii/S0747563214003227.

Van Syckle, Katie. "Hooking Up Is Easy to Do (But Pretty Complicated)." *New York*, October 18, 2015.

Vernacchio, Al. *For Goodness Sex: Changing the Way We Talk to Teens About Sexuality, Values, and Health.* New York: HarperColllins, 2014.

———. "How Much Do Teenagers Know About Sex and the Law?" Interview by Steve Inskeep. *Morning Edition.* NPR, September 3, 2015. Accessed September 24, 2015. http://www.npr.org/2015/09/03/4371328 28/how-much-do-teenagers-know-about-sex-and-the-law.

Ward, Jane. "It Turns Out Male Sexuality Is Just As Fluid As Female Sexuality." *The Conversation*, February 2, 2015. Accessed November 2, 2015. https:// theconversation.com/it-turns-out-male-sexuality-is-just-as-fluid-as-female -sexuality-36189.

Weitzman, Elissa R., Toben F. Nelson, and Henry Wechsler. "Taking Up Binge Drinking in College: The Influences of Person, Social Group, and Environment." *Journal of Adolescent Health*, 2003. Accessed April 3, 2015. http:// archive.sph.harvard.edu/cas/Documents/uptake/uptake1.pdf.

The White House Task Force to Protect Students from Sexual Assault. *Not Alone: The First Report of the White House Task Force to Protect Students from Sexual Assault.* The Oval Office of the Vice President and the White House Council on Women and Girls. April 2014. Accessed October 1, 2015. https://www.notalone.gov/assets/report.pdf.

Wiseman, Rosalind. *Masterminds and Wingmen: Helping Your Son Cope with Schoolyard Power, Locker-Room Tests, Girlfriends, and the New Rules of Boy World.* New York: Harmony Books, 2013.

World Health Organization. "Globally, an Estimated Two-Thirds of the Population Under 50 Are Infected with Herpes Simplex Virus Type 1." World Health Organization Media Centre. 2015. Accessed December 20, 2015. http://who.int/mediacentre/news/releases/2015/herpes/en/.

———. "Hepatitis B." World Health Organization Media Centre. July 1, 2015. Accessed January 2, 2016. http://www.who.int/mediacentre/factsheets/ fs204/en/.

———. Department of Reproductive Health and Research, Johns Hopkins Bloomberg School of Public Health/Center for Communication Programs

(CCP). *Family Planning: A Global Handbook for Providers* (2011 update). Baltimore, MD; Geneva, Switzerland: CCP and WHO, 2011.

Wylie, K. R., and Ian Eardley. "Penile Size and the 'Small Penis Syndrome.'" *BJU International*, 2007. Accessed November 2015. http://www.ncbi.nlm.nih.gov/pubmed/17355371.

Your Brain on Porn. "Brain Structure and Functional Connectivity Associated with Pornography Consumption: The Brain on Porn." Your Brain on Porn (YBOP). August 16, 2014. Accessed December 22, 2015. http://yourbrainonporn.com/brain-structure-and-functional-connectivity-associated-pornography-consumption-2014.

———. "Brain Studies on Porn Users." Your Brain on Porn (YBOP). July 31, 2014. Accessed December 23, 2015. http://yourbrainonporn.com/brain-scan-studies-porn-users.

———. "Evolution Has Not Prepared Your Brain for Today's Internet Porn." Your Brain on Porn (YBOP). Accessed December 23, 2015. http://brain1623.rssing.com/chan-10097734/all_p35.html.

INDEX

ABOUT THE AUTHOR

Cindy Pierce is a social sexuality educator who engages students with her message about making healthy choices and navigating cultural pressures. She uses research, expert opinions, and real feedback from today's college students to demystify sex and the hookup scene. Cindy encourages students look more closely at the way alcohol, social media, gender stereotypes, porn, and skewed expectations are impacting their social lives and sexual relationships. She is the author of *Sexploitation: Helping Kids Develop Healthy Sexuality in a Porn-Driven World* and coauthor of *Finding the Doorbell: Sexual Satisfaction for the Long Haul.* Cindy lives with her family in New Hampshire.